PRE-TRIAL SERVICES AND THE FUTURE OF PROBATION

Pre-trial Services and the Future of Probation

MARK DRAKEFORD, KEVIN HAINES,
BEV COTTON and MIKE OCTIGAN

UNIVERSITY OF WALES PRESS • CARDIFF • 2001

British Library Cataloguing-in-Publication Data.

A catalogue record for this book is available from the British Library.

ISBN 0–7083–1643–3 *1003059560*

Typeset at University of Wales Press
Printed in Great Britain by Dinefwr Press, Llandybïe

For John Drakeford

Contents

Acknowledgements

This book has been made possible through research funding provided by the Association of Chief Officers of Probation and the University of Wales. Our thanks are due to both organizations for their essential assistance.

Our particular thanks are due to Richard Green, assistant chief probation officer, West Midlands, whose own commitment to pre-trial work has made him both a constant source of knowledge and a vital broker in smoothing the path of access to others. Richard chaired the Steering Group which oversaw the research at different stages, and we were grateful throughout for the help which members of the Group were willing to provide.

The chapters which follow record a great deal of practical work conducted at a wide variety of locations and involving a large number of different individuals. We have been struck by the consistent willingness with which individuals at all levels within the Probation Service have given of their time and interest to the study. It is, we hope, a sign of the commitment, actual and latent, which exists within the Service to pre-trial services. We are glad to record our thanks to them all.

Finally we wish to place on record our acknowledgement of the patience and understanding displayed by staff of the University of Wales Press. Dealing with a text in which four different authors are involved produces additional complications, above and beyond those which are inherent in any book production. The help which we have received at all stages from Press staff has been greatly appreciated by us all.

Over the last decade, the politics of criminal justice have become as complex and disputatious as any debate over policy or practice. This book argues for a particular direction in the future of probation. The responsibility for the strength or otherwise of that argument remains, as ever, entirely that of the authors.

Abbreviations

ABH	Actual bodily harm
ACPO	Assistant chief probation officer
CJA	Criminal Justice Act
CJPO Act	Criminal Justice and Public Order Act
CPO	Chief probation officer
CPS	Crown Prosecution Service
CRAMS	Client Record Administration and Management System
DPP	Director of Public Prosecutions
GBH	Grievous bodily harm
HMIP	Her Majesty's Inspectorate of Probation
KPI	Key Performance Indicators
NACRO	National Association for the Care and Resettlement of Offenders
PACE Act	Police and Criminal Evidence Act
PO	Probation officer
PSR	Pre-sentence report
PTS	Pre-trial services
SPO	Senior probation officer
WMPS	West Midlands Probation Service

I. Introduction

This book considers the future of the Probation Service in England and Wales. While there has been no shortage of debate and speculation about that future, the account offered here differs in one crucial respect. It concentrates upon a neglected theme in contemporary practice and policy-making, one which, it is argued here, deserves to occupy a far more central position in the unfolding pattern of criminal justice. While attention focuses upon how the system should deal with those individuals who admit to committing offences, or who are found guilty of doing so, the fate of those who, in huge numbers, are drawn within the same system while awaiting the outcome of charges brought against them is far more neglected. Yet arguments of principle and practicality combine to suggest that a forceful concentration needs to be brought to bear in this direction. At the sharpest end, thousands of individuals are held in custody each year, in some of the worst conditions in British jails, awaiting outcomes which will find them not guilty of any offence, or result in forms of non-custodial sentencing. This book considers ways in which a proportion of these individuals could be held safely in the community during this pre-trial period. Drawing on original research conducted within existing schemes, it argues that the Probation Service already possesses a body of knowledge and experience which, if generalized, could contribute significantly to that end.

Many players are involved in the whole set of decisions which lead up to a final determination of a bail application. Some – the police and the courts – have direct decision-making powers in this regard. Others – such as the Crown Prosecution Service and defence solicitors – are influential actors. This book argues for a strengthened role for the Probation Service in this arena. Of course, change in any one part of a complex system inevitably requires or produces changes in other dimensions. At different points in the chapters which follow we refer to the consequences of a renewed role for probation upon others involved in the bail and remand field. Our focus, however, remains upon the Probation Service itself, attempting to establish the case for a more powerful place for pre-trial work within its own portfolio, and for the centrality of that work within remand management as a whole. In that sense, the audience for this book is a wide one, encompassing the range of services which are involved in this aspect of criminal justice. Our primary concern, however, has been to provide a text which will be directly useful to those who have the responsibility for the design and delivery of probation services and for shaping those services in the future.

The Probation Service has been in a state of flux for at least a quarter of a century. During that period it has been regarded by government both as central and pivotal to its criminal justice plans, and as peripheral and dispensable. A change of government in 1997 which, whatever reservations have been expressed, led generally to a renewed emphasis upon the importance of public services – in health, education and in the social services – has had a different impact in criminal justice. Here, the policies embraced by the new Home Secretary, Jack Straw, had far more in common with those of his predecessor, Michael Howard, than was apparent in any other great department of state. For the Probation Service this has meant continuing uncertainty and a clear sense that the Home Secretary is a more critical than constructive friend of its endeavours.

This book does not set out to resolve all the tensions which lie at the heart of this contested terrain. It does, however, explore one part of the field where, as we finally conclude, reinvigorated activity could combine a respect for core probation values; an enhanced service to the courts; a contribution to the government's agenda of the safe continuation of individuals in the community rather than in custody; and the safeguarding of the essential rights of individual citizens to be treated as innocent until proven guilty, to be presumed worthy of bail until prosecutors can establish otherwise and to organize a defence in conditions which do not make that a practical impossibility.

This framing of our conclusions is, of course, essentially one which emphasizes the arguments of principle which can be invoked in favour of pre-trial services. It is important to be clear that, in conducting the research reported in this book, we began from a basic position of enthusiasm for the advantages which a new approach to this period in the criminal justice process might bring. It is equally important, however, to stress that any conclusions as to the practical possibilities of realizing such advantages arose from, rather than preceded, the research which is reported in the central portion of this book. Four key purposes underpinned the work carried out in exploring the potential for creating a vigorous and effective set of pre-trial services in the contemporary criminal justice process.

Firstly, to make some estimate of the present scale of pre-trial services (PTS) in England and Wales and, in particular, to establish whether such services had grown or diminished since the last full investigation of their prevalence in 1998 (Haines and Octigan 1998). If an in-principle case for pre-trial services could be established, the practical possibility of their extension would depend upon a sufficiently robust existing network – an acorn, at least, from which a larger oak might be grown.

Secondly, to investigate the nature and quality of existing services in this field. Even if a network of services already existed, its capacity to deliver the benefits suggested would depend upon its quality and the generalizability of those qualities which make for success.

Thirdly, to estimate the potential impact of a revived pre-trial capacity upon the current decisions made at the remand stage and to arrive at some preliminary notion of the financial implications of extended capacity. Even if it seemed possible to create a new network of quality services, there would be little incentive to do so if it could not be shown that such a network would be capable of delivering practical and financial benefits.

Fourthly, to estimate the level of support within the service for such an initiative. Even the best of ideas can founder if, for whatever reason, they evoke little sympathy or enthusiasm from those charged with putting them into practice. Our aim was to explore the climate towards pre-trial ideas within the Probation Service, particularly amongst opinion leaders, in order to establish the level of support or otherwise which exists for developing such work in the future.

This text provides an account of our investigation of these four key themes. Exploration begins with a brief history of pre-trial work, both in Britain and in the United States. The American experience is important both because – as so often in recent criminal justice policy – that experience has proved highly influential in generating and shaping initiatives in England and Wales and because lessons remain to be learned from the way pre-trial schemes have developed there. Within England and Wales, too, a history has developed of pre-trial work – short, hesitant, characterized by brief highs and rather more extended lows, but remarkably tenacious in retaining a grip upon the enthusiasm of a group of policy-makers and practitioners even in the least favourable circumstances. Chapter 2 charts this history, drawing particularly upon a Probation Service-wide survey of work carried out by Kevin Haines and Mike Octigan in 1998. From this base line the chapter provides an assessment of the current health of pre-trial work in England and Wales, both in terms of its present scope and in terms of its preparedness to learn some of the lessons of its own history and of the lessons which might be drawn from the American experience.

Chapter 3 moves to an account of some of the original work conducted during the present research. In addition to securing some notion of the scale of pre-trial services, we have aimed to look in detail at actual practice in a range of different settings. Three different probation areas were approached and, in common with the co-operation which the research has met in all its different facets, each one agreed to take part in the work. The areas were chosen on the basis of the differences they could provide in terms of geographical characteristics – urban/rural, density/sparsity and so on – and in terms of internal organization. The chapter aims to provide an account of the range of different activities which are currently conducted under the pre-trial services umbrella and to analyse the strengths and weaknesses which are to be found amongst them. In doing so, the chapter considers a range of different factors, including organizational – the difference, for example, between in-house services and those provided through partnership arrangements – and professional. Practical issues, such as finance and training, emerge as significant, as do systemic questions, in the sense of relations with other key players in the criminal justice process. Most importantly of all, in terms of the central questions posed at the start of the study, this part of the research concludes clearly that a body of well-constructed, carefully evidenced and successfully implemented practice already exists in the pre-trial field. This in turn, however, raises a question which, we would argue, is of real importance, not only in relation to the present research, but is also one which raises more general issues in relation to contemporary policy-making and implementation. We refer here to the short-term and 'project' mentality which has prevailed not only in the criminal justice field, but across the range of public-sector functions. Successive governments, drawn by the need for 'quick wins' at modest expense, have favoured demonstration projects and time-limited funding. The social science research literature is equally stacked with a wealth of 'evaluations' of such initiatives brought about, it often seems, by the on-going struggle by projects to secure funding for their own continuation. The rationale for central government's approach is that, once in place, local organizations will pick up the responsibility for the continuation of initiatives which have demonstrated their own worth. The falsity of this premise can be demonstrated from within the direct history of the Probation Service's involvement in pre-trial work, as chapter 2 sets out. Even where demonstration schemes might have a fair hope of success, however, they remain vulnerable to a further major difficulty, that of mainstreaming the gains which projects might have achieved. This chapter therefore aims, also, to identify those key lessons which need to be learned in any effort to generalize the best local experience on a wider basis.

As well as success on their own terms, as suggested earlier, the most thriving pieces of individual work are unlikely to produce a more general impact unless they meet important objectives within the wider policy environment. Chapter 4 sets out to investigate this aspect of the research, looking at the practical and financial consequences of an extended network of pre-trial services. Amongst the research issues with which this chapter is engaged are the basic ones of data reliability, accessibility and generalizability. Criminal justice agencies collect and store information on a grand scale, with a plethora of different purposes in mind. Yet, as the chapter demonstrates, at a time of global information super-highways, the remand system remains, in large part, locked in the age of Stephenson's *Rocket*, and more or less as reliable, and the methodological challenges of making dependable sense of the emerging picture are considerable. Nevertheless, using those items of information and those analytical tools which are available, a number of noteworthy conclusions are reached. On the basis of a systems approach, the key finding to emerge is that an England and Wales-wide pre-trial service would be capable of contributing to safer and more just decisions at this stage in the criminal justice process, and of doing so in a strikingly economical fashion.

The book then provides a chapter which reports a fourth main strand in the research effort. One of the abiding themes of social welfare development lies in the importance, for their success or otherwise, of the *spirit* as well as the substance in which new ideas are introduced and implemented. Even apparently good ideas can flounder if they fail to capture the support of those entrusted with their application. The views reported here are those of leading figures, drawn from a wide range of probation interests. While differences of emphasis and understanding do emerge, the most striking characteristic of the responses lies in the enthusiastic support for the notion that pre-trial services should be developed and moved towards the centre of the criminal justice stage over the years ahead.

2. The History and Development of Pre-trial Services

The survival of ambivalence

Freddy is remanded in custody charged with burglary. He has been on remand for a considerable number of weeks and is unlikely to be released in the near future. His lawyer has made only one fleeting bail application and will not make another one until a determination of guilt or innocence because Freddy's domestic circumstances are problematic and he thinks that, for the time being, Freddy is better off where he currently is. Traditionally, the Probation Service does not intervene until there is a finding of guilt, and a bail information service does not exist. Freddy is eventually conditionally discharged at the Crown Court for a lesser offence six months later, leaving the system through the perpetually revolving door. During his time on remand Freddy has lost his accommodation, been locked up for twenty-three hours each day and suffered the regular pressures of prison life. He has suffered invasions of privacy each time he was searched and has been subject to a constant sense of danger from some of those incarcerated with him. All of this, before ultimately receiving a sentence reserved for those posing little risk to the public.

Freddy's case exemplifies the barren judicial wasteland that existed between arrest and trial before specific services to divert alleged offenders from a remand in custody were introduced. Historically, amongst court personnel a sense of remoteness, uncertainty, even institutionalized ambivalence seemed to exist in respect of people appearing before the criminal justice system who frequently served prison sentences in advance of any finding of guilt or innocence. There have been major developments in the field of diversion in the last twenty years, but some would argue that this ambivalence remains. Over 60 per cent of people remanded in custody are ultimately not proceeded against, are found not guilty, or receive a non-custodial sentence (Penal Affairs

Consortium 1995a). More disturbingly, in the case of women, that figure is 75 per cent.

This chapter is about the history and development of pre-trial services – in particular, the provision of bail information, bail support and bail hostels. We begin with a definition of pre-trial services: what they are and their purpose. This is followed by a short section on the history of bail to give the reader an insight into the development of bail law and the context within which pre-trial services operate. After this, there is a section on the recent history of remand management, looking especially at the reasons why the remand population has grown relentlessly in recent years, and focusing on the development of pre-trial services to offset this prison growth. There is then a section on the legal path that a defendant will travel on from 'suspect to trial'. Following this we look at pre-trial service developments in the 1990s, commenting on the available research evidence that exists in respect of them, before concluding with some thoughts about the future direction of these services. The chapter ends with a brief history of pre-trial developments in the United States of America, designed to illuminate both the origins of thinking in this field and to suggest some ways in which trends in this area might develop in the future.

What are pre-trial services?

Managing the remand population
Pre-trial services include all those services between arrest and trial that seek to divert defendants from a remand in custody, for example:

- bail information
- bail support
- specific bail conditions (including the electronic monitoring of bailees)
- mental health diversion schemes (at the police station, in court or in custody)
- probation hostels and other offender accommodation usually offering support services and the imposition of a curfew.

Pre-trial services, therefore, primarily exist to offer an alternative to a custodial remand. Firstly, they do this by supplying bail information, which is the provision of value-added information, that would otherwise be unknown, to the court in assisting the bail adjudication. Secondly, by providing bail support or bail accommodation schemes, which directly address the objections to bail that the Crown Prosecution Service (CPS) is mindful to make before the court. Thirdly, through the provision of bail hostels, which offer staff support and supervision together with curfew conditions, and thus operate as a semi-institution located between prison and the community.

Before we look at the nature, purpose and provision of pre-trial services it is important first to contextualize them within the history and development of bail law.

A brief history of bail

Magna Carta to Human Rights Charter

For 600 years, following the signing of Magna Carta in 1215, there was a presumption of bail for defendants appearing before the courts on a charge of misdemeanour (Smartt 1997): 'No free man shall be taken or imprisoned or dispossessed or outlawed or punished or any way be destroyed . . . except by the legal judgement of his peers or by the law of the land' (Magna Carta, 1215, clause 39, quoted in Cavadino and Gibson 1993). The Habeas Corpus Act of 1679 'secured the presence of the body of a person named in writ before the court' (Smartt 1997). This remains an important safeguard against unlawful imprisonment to this day, and this general right to bail remained intact until the nineteenth century. In the nineteenth century there was a series of legislative and judicial decisions that served to diminish that overriding principle. An Act of Parliament in 1826 saw the first erosion of this premise when it stated that 'if there was a strong presumption of guilt, the defendant should be committed to prison', (7 Geo, IV c. 64, in Smartt 1997). This theme continues right up to the enactment of the 1976 Bail Act, where it states 'in reaching a decision to remand in custody . . . the court may consider . . . the strength of the evidence against the defendant of having committed the offence for which charged' (Bail Act 1976, para. 9, Part 1, Schedule 1).

Under the Indictable Offences Act 1848, this traditional right was further diminished and 'granting of Bail was entirely for the justices discretion' (Smartt 1997). In 1884 Lord Russell attempted to clarify the purpose of bail in the case of *R* vs. *Rose*, describing it not as a punishment but as a means to secure the attendance of the prisoner at a trial (*R* vs. *Rose* (1884), 15 Cox, CC540 (Ashworth 1994)). In the Costs in Criminal Cases Act 1908, the court introduced an appellate system to the granting and withholding of bail, which meant that 'the discretion of the justices to grant or refuse bail was open to review by the superior courts' (Smartt 1997).

Nearly fifty years on, the 'Goddard principles' concerning offending on bail (*R* vs. *Wharton* (1955) Crim. LR 565) had a significant effect on the prison remand population in this century. These principles were intended to deny defendants the opportunity of committing further offences whilst on bail. They were later embodied within the 1967 Criminal Justice Act (which also introduced conditional bail) and were ultimately written into the 1976 Bail Act (Ashworth 1994).

The 1976 Bail Act enshrined the fundamental right to bail, though with a list of exceptions to that right (Cavadino and Gibson 1993). It laid down the main procedures to be followed by courts and others involved in the bail process. Furthermore, it governs the number of 'repeat' applications that can be made by the accused and deals with 'full argument certificates' which form the basis of 'appeal' to the Crown Court.

In the case of unconvicted defendants, if the court is satisfied that there are substantial grounds for believing that the defendant, if released on bail, would

(a) fail to surrender to custody
(b) commit an offence whilst on bail
(c) interfere with witnesses or otherwise obstruct the course of justice

then that defendant need not be granted bail. It is in this area of the 1976 Bail Act, that bail support, bail information and bail hostels operate by offering services that will address these objections to the general right to bail.

In reaching a decision to remand in custody or on bail, the court may consider:

(a) the nature and seriousness of the offence or default and the probable method of dealing with the defendant;

(b) the character, antecedents, association and community ties of the defendant;

(c) the defendant's previous record in respect of fulfilling obligations when granted bail previously;

(d) the strength of evidence against the defendant of having committed the offence for which charged (Home Office 1999a).

Bail towards the millennium

In the last twenty years there has been a succession of further amendments to the legal provisions concerning bail. The Police and Criminal Evidence Act (PACE 1984) dealt with police powers to detain suspects and with magistrates' powers to extend the usual maximum period of police detention beyond thirty-six hours. The 1988 Criminal Justice Act (CJA 1988) detailed the circumstances in which bail applications could be made. It enshrined the principle, established in the Nottingham Justices case (*ex parte* Davies 1981 QB 38), which effectively meant that defendants have a right to two full bail applications before a magistrates court. This legislation was introduced partly because research had indicated that magistrates were loath to allow more than one bail application while solicitors were reluctant to apply for bail unless they were convinced that the application would succeed (Brink and Stone 1988). Further bail applications are then normally made to a judge sitting in chambers.

Under the Bail Amendment Act 1993 the CPS were given powers of appeal, although this legislation is rarely used (Home Office 1999a; Hucklesby 1997a).

The Criminal Justice and Public Order Act 1994 introduced some significant amendments to the general right to bail:

- Under section 25 bail was automatically refused if a defendant was charged with murder, manslaughter or rape (actual or attempted in each case) and had a previous conviction for any of these offences or for culpable homicide, and the defendant was sentenced to imprisonment. Section 25 has now been repealed by section 56 of the Crime and Disorder Act 1998.
- In section 26 the presumption in favour of bail does not apply if the defendant is charged with an indictable offence (or either-way offence) which was allegedly committed whilst on bail.
- Section 27 empowered police custody officers to grant conditional bail to persons charged with an offence.

- Section 29 introduced the power of arrest for failure to answer police bail.
- Finally, section 30 empowered the CPS to apply to a court if bail has been granted but new information has come to light or there has been a change of circumstances. In such an event bail may be withdrawn or additional conditions imposed.

The Crime and Disorder Act 1998 further introduced four new amendments to the law on bail:

- Section (54.1) empowers courts to require any person granted bail to give a surety.
- Section (55) gave courts increased powers to demand forfeiture of a surety.
- Section (54.2) allows courts to impose a condition requiring a defendant to attend an interview with a legal adviser.
- Section (56) provides for a rebuttal of the presumption against bail introduced in section 25 of the Criminal Justice and Public Order Act 1994. This last amendment anticipated the incorporation of article 5 of the Human Rights Convention into UK domestic law under the Human Rights Act 1998. Article 5 emphasizes the right to liberty, and the lack of any discretion under section 25 was clearly in breach of this article.

The law on bail has developed significantly during the last century leading up to the legal watershed of the 1976 Bail Act. This Act attempted to make coherent legal sense of the statutory and case law developments that had evolved during this time. Subsequent bail legislation, during the 1980s, focused on access to bail applications and introduced diversionary services in response to the escalating prison remand population. More recently, in the 1990s, there has been a flurry of bail legislation, much of it in response to public outcries (for example that surrounding 'bail bandits' and the case of Winston Silcott) which has undoubtedly further eroded the principle of a general right to bail . A number of organizational and administrative initiatives have developed alongside these legislative changes and it is to these that we refer in the next section.

Recent history of remand management
The 1970s

In the United Kingdom, the concept of providing independent and verified information in relation to the bail process emerged in the 1970s. The Vera Institute of Justice based in New York pioneered the work, principally because of its experience in developing initiatives of this nature. Moreover, it was deemed appropriate to use an 'alien' agency to effect such a change to the prevailing culture (Smith 1994). The scheme focused on verifying the community ties of defendants, providing securities and securing places in bail hostels. Bail information schemes were set up in sixteen magistrates' courts in response to Home Office Circular 155/75 that encouraged this development 'from existing resources'. This initiative did not gain widespread support, principally because the 1976 Bail Act, together with a Home Office circular on bail (1975) led to a decline in the size of the remand population. This reduction defused any sense of urgency that was around at the time, and little more was heard of these sixteen bail information schemes. Graham Smith also mentioned the Probation Service's sense of ambivalence in becoming involved at the remand stage for reasons related primarily to civil liberties. Moreover, he said that defence lawyers considered bail information to be an intrusion into their territory and possibly a contravention of due process (Smith 1994).

Remand crisis in the 80s

The Bail Act 1976 was a watershed in the history of bail in attempting to codify and make coherent judicial sense of bail legislation and other legal decisions. The effect of the Bail Act and the Home Office circular on bail was that 'the number of untried and un-sentenced prisoners received into custody fell from 68,388 in 1975 to 52,581 in 1978' (Cavadino and Gibson 1993). The average daily number of people on remand in 1978 totalled 5,631. This figure however, more than doubled between 1978 and 1988 to a total of 11,444 (Cavadino and Gibson 1993) and 'a group that constituted a mere 8% of the prison population in 1975 came to constitute 22% of the prison population in the late 1980s' (Ashworth 1994). Moreover, the length of time spent on remand had expanded from '25 days to 56 days' by 1987 (Ashworth 1994) thus exacerbating the problem. Other significant factors, largely to do with the administration of justice, had inflated the remand population. These included increasing delay in the processing of cases and the introduction of advanced disclosure of Crown prosecution documents. In fact, the number of cases going to the Crown Court remained the same, but each of these was taking much longer. Twice as many people were therefore being remanded in custody for twice as long, and there was a vacuum in government policy to combat this.

Bail information and support schemes introduced

In 1986 the Crown Prosecution Service was created. Together with concerns about the escalating remand population, its creation heralded an opportunity for the revival in the concept of bail information. Pilot schemes followed, and by 1988 two advisory committees were in existence. Two members of probation staff, Charles Lloyd and Christine Fiddes were seconded by the Association of Chief Officers of Probation (ACOP) to co-ordinate the expansion of bail information schemes nationally and to provide a national training programme for all bail information staff. During the subsequent years, up until March 1995, 100 first appearance (court-based) and a number of subsequent appearance (prison-based) schemes were established throughout the country, although the actual status of some of these schemes appears to have been more nominal than real. Home Office ring-fenced monies, described as the 'hypothecated grant', financed this process in the magistrates' courts, while the remand schemes were funded mostly from existing prison resources (Home Office 1991; Haines and Octigan 1999; Cavadino and Gibson 1993).

Under section 3, subsection 6, of the 1976 Bail Act, an opportunity was provided for a number of probation services to deliver bail support schemes, under the auspices of conditional bail. A number of probation bail support schemes commenced in the early to mid-1990s in response to pump-priming monies made available under the hypothecated grant and the supervision grant arrangements. The money for bail support was made available pro rata to the size of the probation budget although it was expected that this would be a one-off payment to initiate partnerships in delivering this service. The Home Office, however, offered no immediate guidance or specifications such as a national standard to indicate what shape or form bail support programmes should take. They did, though, engage NACRO to support this initiative for a period of three years. During this time some policy guidelines about bail support were produced and a bail support directory was published (NACRO 1996). The directory included information about schemes for adults as well as young people, while indicating that the number of adult schemes was small.

Other diversionary interventions

The successive Conservative governments of the 1980s and early 1990s introduced a number of other initiatives designed to slow down the growth, if not to reduce the size, of the remand population. Statutory time limits were introduced whereby, if a matter was taking too long to process, the court could reconsider bail after a specific time period had elapsed (section 22, Prosecution of Offences Act 1985; Prosecution of Offences (Custody Time Limit) Regulations 1987; 1988; 1989; 1991). Plans for 100 additional bail hostel bed spaces were announced in 1989 (Fielding and Fowles 1990) after Parliament urged a systematic assessment of bail accommodation, given the rising remand population. The electronic monitoring of bailees was piloted. PICA Schemes (Public Interest Case Assessment) were piloted to assist the CPS in making diversionary decisions on defendants for whom a prosecution was not considered to be in the public interest. Finally, mental health diversion schemes were established in magistrates' courts around the UK, and according to Blumenthal and Wessley (1992), '48 schemes were in existence with another 34 under development'.

In 1992, an action research project (Burrows 1993) was set up and overseen by the Bail Issues Steering Group. It aimed, firstly, to improve the quality, accuracy and timeliness of information available to remand decision-makers. Secondly, it sought to assist them in identifying those defendants who were most likely to offend on bail and thus to reduce offending on bail. Several pilot schemes were initiated around the country, and a 'narrative map' of the bail process was used to follow the progress of bailees through the criminal justice system. This demonstrated that, at key stages of the bail process, crucial information such as antecedents was missing, so hampering police bail decision-making. An interim report was published in 1994 (Burrows et al. 1994), though the final report was not issued until four years later in 1998 (Morgan and Henderson 1998). This report explored the issues surrounding bail decision-making, examined the factors associated with specific remand decisions and identified the types of defendants most likely to offend on bail. We will refer to this in greater detail in the next section.

Prison expansion in the 1990s

Following the implementation of the Criminal Justice Act 1991 there had been a fall in both the average daily prison population (to 41,561 by January 1993) and in the proportionate use of immediate custody (from 15.7 to 11.6 per cent – Haines and Drakeford 1998). The remand population, however, remained high (12,400) notwithstanding the introduction of bail information schemes and some bail support schemes to magistrates' courts across the UK in the early 1990s. There were several reasons for this.

In 1992 two police reports produced by Northumbria and Avon and Somerset Constabularies respectively heightened media attention to offending on bail by giving voice to the 'bail bandits' furore. The validity of this 'research' was questioned for a number of reasons. For example, it included all arrests (and some 'clear-ups' – 41 per cent of the sample in Northumbria) amongst the data, rather than focusing simply upon the ultimate convictions. The Home Office (1992) conducted its own research which suggested that there had not been a significant rise in offending on bail since the last time such a major research project had been conducted in this field in 1978 (Home Office 1978). Nevertheless, the effect of the 'bail bandits' rumpus was palpable and had an impact on the prison remand population at that time. Between 1992 and 1994 the remand prison population rose by almost a quarter from just over 10,000 to 12,400.

Another significant milestone in the expansion of the prison remand population came in October 1993, when Michael Howard became Home Secretary. He reversed the trend established by the 1991 Criminal Justice Act for using prisons only for sexual, violent and other defendants posing a threat to the public, and declared that 'Prison works'. As a result the prison population has been on the increase ever since from 41,561 in January 1993 to an all-time high of 66,500 in July 1998. Furthermore, the Public Order and Criminal Justice Act 1994 reversed the right to bail in some cases whilst denying the right to bail altogether in others. Although 'this hardly affected the number of defendants who had allegedly committed offences on bail who were remanded in custody' (Hucklesby and Marshall 2000), it did lead to increases in the use of conditional bail for defendants 'with a bail history' (Hucklesby and Marshall 2000). Magistrates increased their use of conditional bail, and defendants charged with more serious offences and who had a 'bail history' were more likely to be remanded in custody (Morgan and Henderson 1998). Contrary to earlier government policy the number of bail hostel places was reduced following a government decision in 1993 to close eleven hostels with 270 places and to abandon the planned expansion programme. This decision was made on the basis of the temporary drop in hostel occupancy rates to below 70 per cent in 1993 (Penal Affairs Consortium 1995b).

The hypothecated grant for bail information schemes came to an end in March 1995 and was drawn into mainstream probation funding. Probation committees, therefore, continued to be re-financed to provide bail information, but, there was no indicator to determine how much of this money was actually spent on bail information in subsequent years. Recent research (Haines and Octigan 1999) has recorded a considerable diminution in the nature and number of bail information schemes across the country. As the Prison Service and the Probation Service wrestled with budgetary reductions in the late 1990s (amounting to 29 per cent in the case of the Probation Service) debate took place on what was considered to be the core and the peripheral business in each these services. This resulted in the marginalization of bail information in both.

By the middle of the 1990s a contradictory state of affairs appeared to obtain in respect of the remand population. On the one hand there was obvious public and governmental concern about the rapid rise of the remand population. Indeed, several diversionary initiatives and research projects were mounted to counteract this. On the other hand the criminal justice system was subject to unprecedented populist rhetoric, and the 'prison works' agenda became a cornerstone of the Conservative party's policies at this time. It became an institutional imperative not to appear 'soft' on criminals, and the welfarist principles of the Probation Service were questioned whilst its budgets were reduced. Following the reduction of its income, the Probation Service manifested its historical ambivalence to remand services and most bail information schemes were reduced and many disappeared altogether.

From suspect to trial

When a defendant appears before a magistrates' court he or she will have already spent some time in police custody. By then much of the evidence to secure a conviction will have been obtained. Indeed, 'over half of all suspects who are interrogated either confess or make incriminating statements' (Sanders 1994); therefore, what are the factors at this stage of the criminal justice system that will determine whether a suspect is processed or diverted from proceedings altogether? What do we know about offending on bail, and does this knowledge inform the decision-making of key personnel involved in making bail decisions before a defendant actually appears in court?

Arrest to remand

There are a number of 'key decision gates' that a suspect must pass through before the intervention of pre-trial services. First there is the police decision on the street. The Police and Criminal Evidence Act 1984 states that 'there must be some objective basis for the suspicion'. Jefferson and Walker (1992) commented on the discriminatory aspect of this process (Sanders 1994). Indeed in the wake of the Lawrence inquiry the Metropolitan Police have relaxed their stop-and-question policy in relation to black people 'given that black people make up 5% of London's population yet constitute 16% of all arrests' (Home Office 1988).

Next, in making the decision whether to charge or not, McConville et al. (1991) suggest that in 25 per cent of cases the police take no further action other than a caution. If the police decide to charge, then the suspect can be held for up to twenty-four hours, or up to ninety-six hours if magistrates agree (sections 41–4, PACE). McConville (1991) indicates that the decision to charge is more to do with 'cop culture' than with the balance of evidence available. By this he means the police working rules or prejudices that might cause them to arrest or charge one suspect but not another, even though the evidence against them might appear to be the same. Furthermore 'solicitors do not attend interrogations, and when they do they are usually passive' (McConville and Hodgson 1992). Other observers have noted that many legal representatives at police stations are not qualified (Baldwin 1992; Ashworth 1992). This absence, lack of status or passiveness of legal representatives at the police station is likely have a significant impact on whether a defendant is ultimately granted or denied bail. Once a defendant has been charged with an offence, the custody officer must decide whether to allow or refuse bail. In so doing he or she is principally advised by section 38 of the Police and Criminal Evidence Act 1984, and section 27 of the Criminal Justice and Public Order Act 1994, which allows for police conditional bail. Cavadino and Gibson (1993) advise that it is the decision of the custody officer that is critical in determining whether a defendant is subsequently denied bail by reviewing magistrates' courts. Forty per cent of those arrested and charged are subsequently remanded in custody (Cavadino and Gibson 1993). Following the publication of Burrows (1993) it was hoped that section 27 of the CJPO Act 1994 would have made inroads into this, but Brown (1998) suggests that the power to impose police conditional bail has simply 'net-widened'.

Diversion before court

When a defendant has been held overnight in police custody the case file is passed to the CPS the following morning. The CPS examines it to determine whether there is sufficient evidence for a 'realistic prospect of conviction', and if it is in the public interest to prosecute the case. The CPS, therefore, has an opportunity to overrule any erroneous decisions made by the custody officer. McConville et al. (1991) found, however, that the CPS rarely drops cases on the basis of evidential sufficiency and it was equally reluctant to offer cautions, while 'weaker cases are continued in the often correct expectation of a guilty plea' (Sanders 1994). Although the PICA schemes demonstrated that there was an increase in diversion by simply having the cases assessed (Stone 1989) it is suggested that 'the CPS neither attempts nor wishes to raise consciousness of the issue (diversion) among its personnel, (Sanders 1994). Godson and Mitchell (1991) showed that the influence of the CPS was critical: 'Magistrates granted bail in 98% of cases where the CPS did not oppose it; and where the CPS requested a remand in custody, this was endorsed by magistrates in 79% of the cases.' Whereas Hucklesby (1997b) found that defence lawyers protect their credibility before the court with 'sell-out strategies' that distance them from the client if they do not think that a bail application should be made. McConville et al. (1994) went further by asserting that solicitors 'rank their credibility and status with the court above the interest of their clients'. The decision of the custody officer together with the CPS adjudication ultimately is shown to determine the magistrates' decision either to grant bail or remand in custody: 'Magistrates make decisions on the same criteria as the CPS which inevitably means that they will make the same decisions' (Hucklesby 1997a).

Executive justice?

The developments between arrest and production before a court are significant to the operation of pre-trial services. Once the police have decided to charge, all their adversarial weight is channelled behind that decision, even though it may have more to do with 'cop culture' than evidential sufficiency and the public interest. Most defendants plead guilty (72 per cent in the Crown Court, 78.9 per cent in the magistrates' court – National Audit Office 1989). Sanders (1989) suggests that this is because of a failure of solicitors to be adversarial at the police station, leaving them with little more than mitigation and bargaining in the magistrates' court. If, as the research indicates, the CPS are not overly concerned with diversion, and defence lawyers, or largely unqualified paralegal staff, are more concerned with their credibility than the balance of evidence in respect of bail applications, it is perhaps, unsurprising that so many people remanded in custody are found not guilty and/or ultimately receive a non-custodial sentence. It is important, therefore, that bail information officers view the case file at the initial appearance before a magistrates' court with circumspection. What appears to be 'an open and closed case' may not necessarily be so. Little work will have been done other than to support the decision to charge and refuse bail. Furthermore, the research evidence raises the question: if the Probation Service is unwilling to engage in pre-trial services work, which of the existing criminal justice agencies will undertake to do so? Is this an area of the criminal justice system that will benefit from a stand-alone independent organization, with a tightly defined remit unhindered by historical legacy and other professional motives?

Remand strategy?

The Probation Service, like other criminal justice agencies funded by the public purse, is now considered to be a public protection agency. Once its primary concern was to 'advise, assist and befriend offenders' (1907 Probation of Offenders Act). However, its focus has now shifted to protecting the public, reducing offending behaviour and contributing to community safety (Home Office 1999b). The government expects public protection agencies to fulfil these tasks by utilizing existing research knowledge and focusing on 'what works' in reducing offending. In implementing a remand strategy it is imperative that scarce resources are targeted at those offenders who are likely to offend on bail. We know that certain offenders such as young burglars, car thieves and homeless offenders are much more likely to offend on bail (Morgan 1992; Morgan and Henderson 1998). At the same time employed offenders, offenders charged with assault and fraud, together with those aged over twenty-one years of age, are less likely to offend on bail (Morgan 1992; Morgan and Henderson 1998). Whilst most conditional bail imposed by magistrates is contrary to the legal requirements of the Bail Act 1976, it is very effective in keeping defendants out of trouble (Raine and Willson 1996). Furthermore, specific conditions are effective in dealing with particular types of offenders, for example curfews and burglars (Brown 1998). Information such as this could be utlilized in devising an effective remand strategy that imposed appropriate safeguards on those defendants who are deemed more likely to offend on bail whilst ensuring that the 'net' is not widened to include those who will safely respond to unfettered bail.

But is there a remand strategy, and if so, who is responsible for managing it? Following the publication of Morgan and Henderson (1998) and Brown (1998) the government issued a bail strategy to improve the remand decision-making process and tackle the problem of offending on bail. This strategy called for the following: the speeding-up of the criminal justice process; improving the quality of the remand decision and the targeting of conditional bail; improved enforcement of conditional bail; improving the quality of bail management; effective sanctions against abuse of bail; increased availability of remand places for juveniles. This strategy document is yet to be formally promulgated and remains in abeyance. It makes sensible recommendations, yet no specific individual or agency is given the operational responsibility for ensuring the 'quality of bail management' in the criminal justice system. The Prison Service and the Probation Service have their separate performance indicators to measure success. In the case of the Probation Service, the Home Office has called for increases in safe remands on bail for those on whom it reports (Home Office 1999a) and has introduced a key performance indicator (KPI) for bail information. The KPI is based on customer satisfaction criteria that will measure whether bail information schemes offer value-added information to the CPS (Home Office 1999b). Research has shown that the CPS values bail information (Morgan and Henderson 1998), yet notwithstanding this the CPS is likely to object to bail in over 80 per cent of cases at a subsequent appearance, even when such information is available (West Midlands Probation Service Statistics 1997). Therefore it will be possible for the Probation Service to achieve its KPI without affecting the remand population in the slightest, and there will be no one in a position to expose this and make coherent sense of the remand arrangements. There is little evidence to support the view that bail decisions are currently informed by any of the recent research. Who or what is going to change any of this? Probation Circular 29/2000 appears to recognize this deficiency: 'in the longer term Bail Information may become part of a wider remand management system . . .' (Home Office 2000a). Meanwhile, the Bail Practice Committee, which has been in existence for over ten years and includes representation from all the key criminal justice agencies involved in the bail process, is ideally placed to direct such a remand management system. Although this committee has not met for almost twelve months it is currently being manoeuvred into a strategically incisive position within the new prison/probation management structures. Hopefully, a representative body such as this will bring a level of informed consistency and coherence to the remand process.

Pre-trial services in the 1990s

The next section is directly concerned with the provision of pre-trial services. Here we will attempt to cover the existing research literature in respect of bail information, bail support and bail hostels before concluding with some commentary about the current situation of pre-trial services in the year 2000.

Bail information schemes
Purpose
National Standards 2000 state.

> The purpose of Bail Information provided by probation services is to assist the court by providing to the Crown Prosecution Service (CPS) verified information to add to their factual knowledge of the defendant, including risk of harm to the public, and hence contributing to their representations on bail.

Bail information schemes seek, therefore, to add to the CPS's knowledge about a defendant's circumstances so that the CPS can make a more informed and balanced decision about whether to make application to the court for unconditional bail, conditional bail or a remand in custody.

Originally, bail information schemes only offered 'positive' information, which sought to balance the 'negative' information provided by the police. The revision of the bail information national standard in 1995 addressed this issue by placing a duty on bail information officers to act on information which has implications for public safety (section 8), to inform the CPS when a defendant does not give consent to a bail information interview (section 9), to notify the CPS, the police, social services or health authorities about any information which discloses or emphasizes significant potential risk to the public (sections 14–15), and to inform the court if the bail information officer is aware that the court is being misled (section 16). Although the new standard (2000) maintains the sentiments of sections 14–15, the former responsibilities of sections 9 and 16 have been omitted. This is possibly because section 9 is an incursion into the principle of the general right to bail, while section 16 is implicit.

Pilot schemes
Bail information schemes originated in the USA. In the 1970s attempts were made to introduce them into the UK where, as in the USA, there were growing concerns that too many pre-trial defendants were being detained unnecessarily.

The introduction of the Bail Act in 1976 reduced the remand population to such an extent that the need for bail information schemes diminished. It was only revisited in the middle of the 1980s, by which time the remand population had effectively doubled. The arrival of the CPS in 1986 provided a unique opportunity to pilot an initiative whereby verified positive information could be given to an independent agency charged with the responsibility of assessing whether a defendant was or was not a good bail risk. The task, therefore, was to 'enhance the capacity of the CPS to review the case'. Prior to the introduction of bail information 'the CPS had little, if any, information other than that provided by the police' (Cavadino and Gibson 1993). As we have seen from the previous section, the information provided by the police to the CPS could have more to do with 'cop culture' than a distinct necessity to prosecute or remand in custody.

Hypothecated grant

Following negotiations between ACOP (the Association of Chief Officers of Probation) and the DPP (the director of public prosecutions), four pilot schemes were established in 1987, and at the conclusion of these pilots, the Vera Institute issued a report with five recommendations:

> A single set of guidelines to be agreed with the Crown Prosecution Service and the Probation Service, governing the manner in which Bail Information is provided to prosecutors; compulsory attendance at a national course; full time not integrated schemes – and where integrated schemes are necessary, they should be integrated with tasks other than traditional court work; the provision of adequate resources and the co-ordinated extension of schemes. (Stone 1988)

In the years leading up to 1995, bail information schemes were extended to most magistrates courts. This growth was financed by the 'hypothecated grant', which came to an end in that year. Several remand prisons also established schemes, and in some cases probation-hypothecated grant monies were used for this purpose (Haines and Octigan 1999).

What information?

Bail information schemes seek to interview defendants at risk of a remand in custody in magistrates' courts, and/or those who are remanded in custody at the local remand prison. Information that is commonly sought and provided to the court includes the following:

(a) The availability of appropriate services: these might include medical treatment, mental health services or drug treatment facilities.

(b) Demonstrated reliability: this could involve membership of clubs, associations or others that indicate that a defendant is established within a community and therefore likely to respond to bail.

(c) Good community support: this could be provided by family, friends, church, mosque and so on, and indicates support mechanisms available within the community to sustain, and vouchsafe the defendant whilst on bail.

(d) Supervision history: if the defendant is or has been on probation or under other community supervision, then the bail information officer may be able to verify information concerning the defendant's response to this and thus reassure the court that she or he is likely to surrender to custody.

(e) Hostel placement available; bail information officers spend most of their time arranging places at probation hostels, as the courts often welcome the provision of extra supervision and the possibility of a curfew. A hostel placement can reassure a court in respect of surrendering to custody and, with the use of curfew, reduce the likelihood that the defendant will offend whilst on bail. Moreover, if the defendant lives in close proximity to a witness or indeed the complainant, it is possible to obtain a probation hostel placement well outside the geographical area in order to reduce the prospect of the defendant acting in breach of bail conditions.

(f) Employment/training available: with the consent of the defendant it may be possible to contact an employer to verify employment. As the schemes usually have protocols with employment agencies covering confidentiality, it is possible to ensure the speedy transmission of this information to the courts where appropriate. The provision of a hostel together with full-time employment is often enough to neutralize many substantial objections to the granting of bail.

(g) A verified stable address: simply verifying an address can be enough to secure a remand on bail. In offences of a domestic nature and/or where there remains a possibility that witnesses will be interfered with, the CPS will object to bail unless distance is created between the complainant and the defendant until the matter is resolved by the courts. In situations such as this, and in the case of allegations of sexual assault on children, it is common to seek a probation hostel or an address in another county.

Bail information schemes can provide a considerable amount of relevant information pertinent to a bail application that the CPS would otherwise not know. This information may reassure the CPS that the defendant resides within a particular community and has local ties and responsibilities, so that the grounds for suspecting that a defendant will flee are not met or substantiated.

Service to the CPS?

An effective scheme at a magistrates' court has to work quickly if it is to interview a defendant and verify information concerning her or him, before submitting the verified information to the CPS. There is always a sense of urgency about clearing away the remand decisions in the morning. Doherty and East (1985), for example, found that '38% of Magistrates decisions took less than 2 minutes, and 87% less than 10 minutes'. It is notable that in England and Wales bail information is provided to the CPS and not, as in America, directly to the courts. This is because it is believed that if no information is forthcoming the court may assume that there is nothing favourable to say. It is possible, however, that the CPS may also make this assumption. Lloyd (1992) suggested that the CPS gave bail information schemes a mixed reception, mainly because only positive information was submitted, which was seen as largely relevant to the defence. Now that bail information schemes reveal 'negative' information about, for example, a defendant's response to supervision, or public protection information that the court would otherwise not know about, some defence lawyers have instructed their clients not to be interviewed by officers from the scheme. Moreover, once the CPS has objected to bail at an earlier court appearance where bail information was provided, it is more than likely to support the earlier colleague's decision at a subsequent appearance, notwithstanding the existence of extra positive information. In one county, for example, 107 bail support orders were made in 1999 on defendants who had been previously remanded in custody. The CPS objected to bail in virtually all of them, preferring, as one Crown prosecutor suggested, 'to allow the courts to make the decision on the balance of the information before it' (Pre-trial Services Steering Meeting 1999). Furthermore, in 1997, the CPS objected to bail in 83 per cent of cases where a bail information report was submitted (WMPS statistics 1997) at a subsequent appearance.

Given that prisons only operate subsequent-appearance schemes, their key customer, the CPS, will usually object to bail in more than four out of five cases when information is duly provided, despite the fact that bail information was considered to be 'very important or quite important' to the CPS in four out of five cases (Morgan and Henderson 1998). Prison governors might well question the efficacy of such schemes, given such stark statistics. The position of bail information officers in the matrix of other key personnel involved in the making of a bail application is therefore uncertain. Defence lawyers are suspicious of 'negative' information, and the CPS appears to be a reluctant customer. Given that bail information officers now offer 'negative' as well as 'positive' information, but the CPS still objects to bail in most cases where a bail information sheet is provided, this service may need to be remodelled, possibly with a view to operating schemes along the same lines as their American models: providing information directly to the court.

Are bail information schemes effective?

> Magistrates would not regularly, if ever, sentence a defendant to imprisonment on the limited information available on a bail application. Yet frequently the question of whether or not to refuse bail has an important influence on the sentence which is eventually passed.
>
> Lord Justice Woolf 1990 (in Cavadino and Gibson 1993)

Following the establishment of bail information schemes in most magistrates' courts across the country by the early 1990s, several research studies were initiated to measure their effectiveness. Godson and Mitchell (1991), reporting on data from bail information schemes in seven magistrates' courts, suggested that 'the CPS requested remands in custody in only 51% of the cases where the police objected to bail but the probation service submitted a bail information sheet, compared with 73% of cases where the police objected to bail but bail information was not provided' (Godson and Mitchell 1991). Additionally they noted a 'halo' effect illuminating the finding that the defence was more likely to make a bail application if a bail information sheet was available. Lloyd (1992) commenting on research at Hull, Manchester and Blackpool magistrates' courts, indicated that bail information had a 'marked effect on CPS decisions in Hull and a substantial effect at Manchester', but the effect at Blackpool was less significant. This report suggested that bail information schemes (BIS) were particularly effective in dealing with the homeless: '72% of homeless defendants who had information presented were bailed compared with 15% where information was not presented' (Lloyd 1992). In Scotland, Warner and McIvor (1994), reporting on schemes in Glasgow and Edinburgh, concluded that bail information had diverted 29 per cent and 19 per cent of defendants respectively who otherwise would have been remanded in custody. In 1992 the effectiveness of bail information was further vindicated when an inspection was carried out by Ann Collyer of the Probation Inspectorate, who concluded that 'bail information schemes have been a significant influence on the CPS's recommendations on the use of bail and are cost effective' (Cavadino and Gibson 1993). All of these studies spoke positively about bail information, and given that its ultimate purpose was to assist the CPS in avoiding unnecessary remands in custody it appeared to be effective.

Looking at prison bail information schemes, Beamer (1991), reporting on the success of the Holloway scheme in diverting women from custody, discovered also that 71 per cent of those who failed to secure bail after the intervention of bail information did not ultimately receive a custodial sentence. The implication was that bail information had the potential to divert still more defendants from Holloway Prison. Williams (1992) reported positively about the success of the Moorland Prison scheme in diverting defendants from custody 'at only marginally greater costs and without associated increases in the proportions of accused who allegedly breach their bail orders'. The impact of bail information was also clearly demonstrated by Nottingham and Mitchell (1994) who surveyed twenty-four prisons: at fourteen of these, between 25 and 49 per cent of prisoners obtained bail where information was provided, and at five prisons the proportion was between 50 and 74 per cent.

Similarly, Home Office Research and Planning Paper no. 46 (Home Office, 1988) involved 323 remands to Wormwood Scrubs contrasted with a control group of 337 remands. This demonstrated that 'more than five times as many of the experimental group than the control group were granted bail'. Murray and Octigan (1997) estimated the cost of the untried remand population to be £184 million. They calculated that the potential combined impact of the actual court-based bail information schemes together with comprehensive bail information cover in remand prisons could reduce the burden of untried remand prisoners by as much as 11.2 per cent. The Probation Inspectorate also visited six prison schemes (Collyer et al. 1993) and found that 'the extent to which prison officers are available to work in the scheme in partnership with the probation service depends on the governor's attitude to such work and/or the tightness of the budget'. The report concluded that 'faced with difficult choices about staff or accommodation resources [governors], had not given sufficient priority to bail information. This had led to failed or failing schemes' (Collyer et al. 1993).

Notwithstanding the effectiveness of these bail information schemes in safely diverting defendants away from a custodial remand, and the considerable financial savings that accrued to the government in the process, their future was not secure. Ring-fenced monies had ensured their establishment in magistrates courts across the country, yet they still appeared to be operating on the fringes of the Probation Service and were not formally a part of the CPS. Some prisons had established schemes out of existing budgets, but the success of these was dependent upon the favourable disposition of prison governors towards them. Prison bail information schemes, like their court counterparts, were detached from the primary business of their own organization, which was concerned with the security of those that they contained. This detachment was to render bail information schemes particularly vulnerable to the budgetary cuts that were imposed on the Prison and Probation Services in the mid- to late nineties.

Bail support schemes

Bail information schemes primarily address the issue of stable accommodation and thus the likelihood of absconding. They can provide information about community ties, which indicate a measure of certainty, consistency and stability in the defendant's life. Bail information schemes do not, however, address the two major reasons for objecting to bail: the seriousness of the offence and the likelihood that the defendant will commit further offences on bail. Bail support schemes of varying intensity, tailored to the needs of the defendant and the court, have been developed in an attempt to fill these needs, and it is to these that this next section refers.

Definition

Bail support schemes across the UK have existed with a variety of definitions usually associated with the local reasons for their genesis. The Penal Affairs Consortium provides the most exhaustive definition:

> Typically in such schemes, an individual bail support programme is arranged specially for each defendant, but schemes generally have one or a number of the following elements: requirements to report, and agreed levels of contact with bail support workers: residence requirements; arrangements for accommodation; contact with volunteer befriending schemes; assistance with education; training; social skills; employment and work placements; monitoring attendance at educational establishments and other activities; helping to resolve family problems and ensuring a continuing home base for the defendant; liaison with agencies providing help with benefits, drug or alcohol misuse, debt counselling, focused individual work addressing such areas as lifestyle, anger management, gambling, budgeting, reparation and peer group influences, programmes of activities to make constructive use of leisure time; and the development of community ties. (Penal Affairs Consortium 1995b).

In *Managing Remand* (NACRO 1995) bail support is considered to operate at three levels. Firstly, offering a voluntary and non-statutory service to the court in assisting the defendant to comply with any bail conditions imposed. Secondly, offering a range of services, usually to offset a remand to a local authority, under the aegis of the Children Act 1989. Thirdly, intervening on a statutory basis under section 3 (6) of the Bail Act 1976. This involves the imposition of specific conditions necessary to ensure that the defendant surrenders to custody, does not commit an offence whilst on bail, does not interfere with witnesses or otherwise obstruct the course of justice, or is available for the purpose of inquires or a report. A bail support programme may address one or all four of these heads. There is no requirement for the justices to find 'substantial grounds' for the imposition of conditional bail; the test is 'is the condition necessary?' for example, 'to prevent the commission of an offence' (Cavadino and Gibson 1993).

NACRO (1993) suggests that bail support is characterized particularly by its diversity: 'some provide accommodation, some do not; some offer a voluntary package whilst others make bail support an explicit condition of bail with intensive day-care programme.' The paper argues for greater consistency in the underlying principles of bail support and for a common approach to the assessment of particular needs and to the location of that assessment within the legislative framework. Ashworth (1992) concurs with this sentiment calling for 'a new middle path between custodial remand and conditional bail . . . with properly funded supervision from the Probation Service'.

NACRO (1993) argues that bail support conditions 'must be purposeful . . . to save some people being kept in prison and not to burden those who will in any event be granted bail by the adding of conditions'. The conditions attached to bail should be designed to overcome the 'substantial grounds' for denying bail and must address the specific circumstances of the denial. When offering a bail support programme to the court, the proposer should therefore bear in mind the following: the gravity of the offence and probable sentence; the character, antecedents, associations and lack of community ties of the defendant; any record of previous breaches of bail conditions; any anticipated lack of co-operation for the purpose of obtaining a report; and the behaviour towards and proximity to prosecution witnesses.

A variety of schemes

Several bail support Schemes emerged during the early 1990s in response to 'pump-priming' monies made available under the hypothecated grant and the Home Office Supervision Grants Scheme (the latter grant-aided probation services from April 1992 until April 1995, mainly to provide supportive accommodation). NACRO was commissioned by the Home Office to advise on the development of bail support during the 1990s and produced a number of advisory papers and documents (NACRO 1993; 1994; 1995).

In Hereford and Worcester (NACRO 1994), 'bail support' was considered to be a 'catch all term for the type of resources that probation services, social services departments and voluntary organisations offer to the courts to support defendants during their bail period'. The purpose of this scheme was to target those who would otherwise be denied bail and ensure their safe return for future court hearings. Devon launched a similar scheme in April 1994 (Devon Probation Service 1994). It listed many of the purposes mentioned above, but added, 'addressing the harmful effects of offending behaviour on the community'. This raises the question whether schemes should be doing this with non-convicted defendants. Also included was 'reducing the inappropriate use of statutory hostels and enhancing the abilities of the PSR writers to assess the defendants' response to any community sentences' (Devon Probation Service 1994). This provides those with previously poor responses to community supervision with an opportunity to demonstrate good intentions ahead of sentencing.

The Dorset scheme was evaluated over two years by Southampton University (Pritchard 1996) and 'offered help, friendship and guidance to those aged 17–25 years', living in Bournemouth and released by the local police or magistrates' court on bail. Participation on the scheme was, therefore, voluntary and included 'help with accommodation, income support and housing benefit; information where to go for specialist assistance; help with substance abuse problems; advice about employment and training and how to make creative use of leisure' (Pritchard 1996).

In the West Midlands definition (WMPS 1999), bail support is 'a service offered to the court to support the defendant on bail and to assist the safe return of the defendant to court thereafter in circumstances where bail would not otherwise be granted'. This scheme targets those already remanded in custody and often makes applications to a judge in chambers as a 'change in circumstances' after two previous refusals of bail at the lower court. The WMPS scheme offers, at one end of the continuum, a regular escort service to court for those defendants not considered to be a risk to the public but who have and are likely to fall foul of their bail conditions; and, at the other, a multifaceted programme which may involve a hostel, a training scheme, drugs counselling, weekend activities, together with an escort to court for those defendants considered to present some risk to the public and/or likely to offend on bail. Judges in the West Midlands have also granted a number of bail support orders in chambers where the principal objection is related to the serious nature of the offence. Many of these orders have been supervised for over twelve months, and the outcomes have often resulted in reduced charges, acquittals or a non-custodial sentence. It appears therefore that bail support can provide reassurances to the court and to the public where the offence is considered serious, but the outcome is likely to be tempered with understanding and mercy.

Financing bail support
The great majority of probation services which provided bail support did so with monies provided, as referred to earlier, by the hypothecated grant scheme and the supervision grants scheme (Home Office 1999a). Both schemes were devolved to probation areas in 1995. The NACRO bail support survey revealed that youth justice services had been providing bail support for at least five years, and in many areas it had become an integral part of youth justice services' general remand provision. Unlike in the case of the probation service, historically, a cost benefit has accrued to local authorities that provided bail support if it offsets the price of a remand into care. The Royal Philanthropic Society, for example, costed their bail support service at £102 per week, compared with £588 per week for residential care provided directly and £1,000 for a residential placement in the local or private or voluntary sector (NACRO 1996). Bail support for young offenders is now funded through the Youth Justice Board.

There is no such cost benefit for the Probation Service; rather bail support incurs costs on the Probation Service which provides resources for defendants who would otherwise be accommodated by the Prison Service. The cost of the WMPS bail support scheme, for example, was estimated at £90 per week (per defendant) as opposed to £388 and £470 per week for men and women respectively remanded in custody (WMPS 1999). WMPS now indicates that pre-trial services will be targeted at those things for which the service is judged. The Home Office has no criteria against which to judge the success of probation services in providing bail support. It remains to be seen whether WMPS believes that it is funded for bail support or whether continued provision depends upon additional Home Office funding or the introduction of a key performance indicator for bail support.

Are bail support schemes effective?
Given that bail support schemes have evolved at different times, and can vary in terms of purpose, target group, programme

content and so on, it is not easy to demonstrate effectiveness, either in cost terms or reoffending terms in an uniformly comparable way. Nevertheless questions one might ask in determining the effectiveness of bail support schemes are:

- Did this defendant abscond/appear at court?
- Did the defendant keep their job/accommodation?
- Would this defendant otherwise have been in custody?
- Did this defendant offend on bail, or offend less often on bail?
- Was this individual treated for any addictions, which reduced her or his offending behaviour?
- Did the defendant maintain family responsibilities and offset any costs to the local authority if children have been taken into care following the remand of a carer?

More fundamentally:

- Was bail support used appropriately?
- Was it necessary?
- Did it occupy the gap between conditional bail and custody?
- Was it cheaper than its prison alternative?

Assessing the effectiveness of bail support schemes is thus complicated and needs to take into account the overall aims and objectives of the individual schemes.

Some measures of effectiveness

Some projects have attempted cost-benefit analyses, usually comparing their costs with those of remand prisons. WMPS, for example, targeted defendants after the second remand in custody. In 1996/7, fifty-two orders were made, and of these, time on the scheme varied from one day to forty-five weeks. Defendants' previous convictions ranged from none to forty. Offence allegations ranged from shoplifting to murder. A total of 83 per cent of defendants concluded their time on the WMPS bail support programme without reoffending (WMPS 1997), providing the cost savings reported above.

Dorset Probation Service offered voluntary intervention together with general advice about a range of issues that might contribute to offending on bail. Pritchard (1996) did a cost-benefit analysis of the Dorset schemes starting from the hypothesis that each crime costs the taxpayer £2,700. He estimated that the successful diversion of 300 heroin-dependent people in east Dorset would provide savings for the criminal justice system amounting to £2,737,500.[1] He suggested that this estimate erred on the conservative side. Conversely, he argued that we could abandon any notion of rehabilitation and send them all to prison, which in the case of east Dorset would cost the taxpayer £62,188,000.[2] This was apart from prison's poorer rate of recidivism compared with probation. This scheme was subsequently withdrawn owing to a reduction in the overall funding of the Dorset Probation Service.

Devon Probation Service focused on reducing offending behaviour, rationalizing the use of statutory hostels and the contribution to the quality of PSRs as criteria to judge the success of their bail support programme. These three specific variables (Did the bailees reduce their offending behaviour? Were statutory hostels not used because of the existence of the scheme? Did added information go into PSRs and improve their quality) would have been the central focus for an evaluation of this scheme. Unfortunately, this scheme was closed in 1998, following budgetary reductions, before it could be properly evaluated.

In Northamptonshire (Northamptonshire Probation Service 1996), the bail support scheme demonstrated that bail was granted after the second remand in custody in 70 per cent of applications made. Of these, 92 per cent completed the bail support programme successfully without reoffending. This scheme, despite its measured success, was also subsequently terminated when the Northampton Probation Service had its overall budget reduced.

Between April and November 1994, fifty-five defendants were placed on the Leeds adult bail support scheme run by the West Yorkshire Probation Service. All had previously been remanded in custody and were bailed to the scheme at a subsequent court appearance following a judge in chambers application. The majority 'completed a Bail Support Scheme successfully' and just six committed further offences during the bail period (Penal

---

[1]   Pritchard came to this conclusion by the following equation:
£25 per gram of heroin × 365 days × 300 heroin users = £2,737,500.

[2]   He came to this conclusion by the following equation:
£28,000 (prison cost) × 2,221 (heroin users) = £62,188,000.

Affairs Consortium 1995). This scheme was also terminated owing to budgetary reductions in the West Yorkshire Probation Service.

Merseyside Probation Service, in conjunction with the John Paul Getty Foundation, has delivered bail support schemes to identified drug offenders since January 1995 (Murray and Octigan 1997). In 1997 the scheme was recognized by the Department of Health as an example of innovative inter-agency co-operation. Since April 1997 three area health authorities have funded the scheme, in addition to ongoing finance provided by Merseyside Probation Service. In 1996, 414 proposals were placed before the court. One hundred and thirty were bailed to the programme following a remand in custody. Of these, sixty-seven were completed success-fully, twenty-four were ongoing (when the information was gathered) and thirty-eight were either breached, had absconded or were arrested. As a successful pioneering scheme it was later chosen as one of the pilot schemes for the drug treatment and testing programme introduced by the Crime and Disorder Act.

In 1993, Powys Probation Service introduced a scheme, which became operational across the whole county by June 1994. The Powys scheme stands as a beacon of anti-discriminatory practice to those smaller urban probation areas who have not delivered a scheme because of arguments premised upon budgets and numbers. This scheme has a judicious mix of full-, part-time and voluntary staff. From a budget of £23,318 in 1997/8 the scheme anticipated 500 interviews costing £46.63 per interview. The scheme supervised thirty-six orders in 1997, of which six were breached, twenty received non-custodial sentences, and the rest were awaiting the outcome of court proceedings. Three defendants were known to have offended on bail. The unit cost of each bail support order was £320.

From the limited information that is available on bail support it would appear that these schemes have been effective at targeting appropriate referrals. And when information is available there has been little evidence of offending on bail. What is also revealed is that most of the probation bail support schemes were ultimately closed down, though not because they were ineffective. Far from it. The reason was to be found in financial pressures.

A number of adult bail support schemes, therefore, emerged in the early 1990s in response to monies made available under the hypothecated and supervision grant schemes. Most of these schemes were statutory, being perceived as an alternative to a remand in custody, and derived their authority from section 3 (6) of the Bail Act 1976. A number of evaluative reports have demonstrated that these schemes were effective both in terms of reoffending rates and the relative costs of a custodial remand. Pre-trial services research (Haines and Octigan 1999) uncovered the general ambivalence this area of work faces within the Probation Service nationally. This is particularly seen in the absence of a remand strategy in most Probation Service action plans. It is therefore unsurprising that when budgetary reductions were made in the latter part of the 1990s, amidst the 'prison works' sloganing, that most of the bail support schemes disappeared. Following the return of a Labour government and the replenishment of probation budgets, it is somewhat disappointing that there has been no attempt to resurrect these schemes.

Budgetary cuts
When the hypothecated grant ceased in 1995, the total pre-trial services budget was taken into mainstream funding. Pre-trial services were therefore one of a series of budget heads that were argued over in a context of an 'hierarchy of importance' for the Probation Service at the end of each financial year. 'De-hypothecation', as it was termed, also coincided with savage budgetary cuts to the Probation Service (predicted to be 29 per cent by the year 2000), alongside a record increase in incarceration that was not accompanied by concomitant resource increases for the Prison Service. Pre-trial services budgets were considerably reduced, and in some cases, disappeared altogether within probation services (in the West Midlands the pre-trial services annual budget was reduced by £250,000 – Haines and Octigan 1999) and within the Prison Service the prevailing mentality of security overshadowed the significance of bail information. The ambivalence and lack of ownership of bail information by either the Probation Service or the Prison Service appeared to manifest itself most acutely at the point of crisis. When the chips were down, when the money was running out and when increasing demand was bearing down on a diminishing resource, the first thing that appeared to go was the area of work that neither organization considered to be within its tradition. The hypothecated grant was no longer ring-fenced, the national bail information co-ordinator

had moved on, and there was no specific individual within the Home Office responsible for the maintenance and continuation of bail information. This occurred at the height of the Home Secretary Michael Howard's 'remoralization' and 'prison works' (Wilson and Ashton 1998) campaign, and any outcries about diversion schemes disappearing would have been largely muted by the imperative to demonstrate the effectiveness of prison in reducing crime. In 1994 Michael Howard had claimed a 5.5 per cent drop in the crime rate, the biggest fall for forty years, as vindication of this policy. Any protests from the Probation Service would probably have been tempered by threats that existed at the time to its very existence (Wilson and Ashton 1998).

Probation hostels
According to National Standards 2000 the purpose of approved bail hostels is to:

> provide an enhanced level of residential supervision with the aim of protecting the public by reducing the likelihood of offending. Approved hostels are for bailees, probationers and post custody licensees, where their risk of causing serious harm to the public or other likelihood of re-offending means that no other form of accommodation in the community would be suitable. (Home Office 2000b)

Bail hostels therefore are to be used as an alternative to custody. Bail hostels can keep people in employment; maintain links between defendants and their families; confront offending behaviour; repair damaged relationships; prepare defendants for independent living in the event of a finding of not guilty or the imposition of a community sentence. They encourage defendants to take responsibility for themselves. When remanded in custody, a defendant's entire life is structured for him or her, often involving confinement in the cell for up to twenty-three hours each day. More ominously, the suicide rate of prisoners on remand is high.

Probation hostels, which have been in existence since 1927, were originally intended for defendants with 'environmental difficulties' (Hardy 1997), and by 1966 there were twenty-one in existence. The first bail hostel was a wing of a Salvation Army hostel and opened in 1971 (Simon and Wilson 1975) before bail hostels were financed by provisions in the 1972 Criminal Justice Act to be used as an alternative to a custodial remand. They were placed on a statutory footing by the Powers of the Criminal Courts Act 1973 and are now available on a nationwide basis, although provision is affected by the priorities of local probation committees (Payne 1989). By 1993 there were thirty bail hostels providing 659 bail beds in addition to eighty-four probation hostels catering for an array of offenders, 63 per cent of whom were bailees (Cavadino and Gibson 1993). The Home Office annual report of 1993 envisaged an expansion of bail beds to 3,190 by the end of 1994/5. As mentioned earlier in this chapter, in 1993 this policy was reversed by the incoming Home Secretary, Michael Howard. Eleven hostels were closed and the number of bed spaces reduced from 2,735 to 2,421, of which 73 per cent were occupied by bailees (Penal Affairs Consortium 1995). This was partly in response to a temporary period of under-occupancy and publicity given to local hostility that existed with some hostels (Collyer et al. 1993). Subsequently, Bennetto (1994) has reported occupancy levels of 84 per cent. WMPS Central Bail Referral Scheme has reported constant overloading of referrals between 1996 and 2000, to the effect that on over 2,000 occasions it has been unable to provide a bed (even though WMPS accept four referrals for every bed that is available).

Are bail hostels effective?
The available research on offending on bail at bail hostels is encouraging. In WMPS in 1992, only 8.9 per cent of bailees were known to have offended on bail. In Manchester only 7.5 per cent were rearrested or charged with an offence, and in Inner London only 6.6 per cent committed an offence whilst at a hostel (Cavadino and Gibson 1993). These figures compare well with research by Morgan (1992), which estimated that 9–12 per cent of bailees offended on bail.

According to the Home Office Research and Planning Unit (1990), 75 per cent of offenders at bail hostels are there for theft and burglary, whilst 20 per cent have allegedly committed an offence of violence. Whether hostels are used as an alternative to custody, the impression is variable. White and Brodie (1980) were clear that this was the case, whilst Pratt and Bray (1985) disagreed, suggesting that many bailees found themselves at hostels un-necessarily because solicitors were 'playing safe'. Lewis and Mair (1988) were uncertain, but suggested that such a 'malfunction' might exist (Ashworth 1992). Internal inspection reports in WMPS have questioned the 'riskiness' of a certain number of hostel-dwellers, whilst highlighting the difficulties in referring drug addicts and mentally disordered offenders (WMPS 1999). This is not a new problem; the Home Office Research and Planning Unit (1988) reported that 'hostels are not willing to take such cases'. Other audits of offender accommodation providers (WMPS 1999) demonstrated that this is also true of other accommodation providers. Moreover, there has been a dramatic reduction in the availability of such accommodation, often called landlady schemes, since reductions in housing benefit were introduced in 1998.

Hostels and equal rights

Women constitute approximately 4 per cent of the prison remand population (Cavadino and Gibson 1993). As a consequence, the limited hostel provision is seldom local. Mixed accommodation is available in a number of hostels nationwide. However, much of this is deemed inappropriate for many of these women, who have often suffered abuse at the hands of men. Even in urban areas women find themselves remanded in custody because of the paucity of appropriate accommodation and services to meet their particular needs. At Birmingham magistrates' court in 1999 bail information officers subsequently interviewed virtually all of the women who were remanded in custody. However, in the majority of cases they were unable to furnish the court with a bail alternative (WMPS 1999).

All bail hostels operate anti-discriminatory policies, yet black people and those from ethnic minorities are largely under-represented in hostels, whilst over-represented in the prison population (Commission for Racial Equality 1990). Local analysis in WMPS has suggested that although the referral process appears non-discriminatory (Hardy 1997), marginally more black/ethnic minority cases refuse the offer of a hostel. When they do, however, agree to a referral, they are less likely to be bailed to a hostel than their white counterparts (WMPS 1999).

Conclusion

We began this chapter by referring to an institutional ambivalence that exists within the British criminal justice system towards the remand prison population. Despite the introduction of numerous research initiatives and other diversionary programmes during the last fifteen years, we would suggest that the situation remains the same. Although recent Home Office developments have been more encouraging, no one person or organization is responsible for the remand population, and consequently the latter is achieved by default rather than by design. Research shows that once a defendant is denied bail at the police station the emphasis is upon securing a conviction, and little energy is devoted to diversion from a remand in custody.

Remand management requires leadership and 'joined-up thinking'. As the current situation operates, a suspect who is arrested and denied bail is proceeded with amidst a constellation of different public protection professionals and agencies which are adversarial in nature and not necessarily functioning from research-based tenets in their decision-making. Worse still, the final bail arbiter, the magistrate, has been found to make wholesale bail decisions that are illegal (Raine and Willson 1996)!

Effective remand services are those that directly address valid police and CPS objections to bail by assessing, and where necessary managing, risk in the community. Ideally they should engage in 'whole-systems thinking' amidst an inter-agency consensus that identifies the people against whom the public needs to be protected, and use proven methods for dealing with defendants. They should do this without losing cognizance of the general principle of a right to bail under the Bail Act 1976. How can we therefore, as public protection agencies, ensure that those who require unconditional bail, conditional bail, bail support, voluntary hostels, supported lodging schemes, statutory hostels, foster care, secure care, electronic tagging, appropriate treatment, or a compound of all of these, receive the intervention that ensures the safety of the public whilst having regard for due process and the legal rights of citizens?

An imperative in all of this is the question of leadership. Unless we define what kind of a remand population we ought to have, it will be determined for us. As we argued previously:

A vision for the future of Remand Services is one in which a fully articulated set of court-focused remand services, firmly located within the public protection and effectiveness agendas, can be mobilised to reduce, wherever possible, unnecessary and inappropriate remands in custody. (Haines and Octigan 1999)

The American experience of pre-trial services[3]

This chapter now turns to a brief overview of the development of pre-trial services in the United States, from their earliest beginnings to the present day. In short compass it is not possible to detail this history for such a large country, with its federal and state systems – and their inherent differences. Nevertheless, an overview of these developments is achievable, and key issues and debates in the growth of pre-trial services will be highlighted. So much criminal justice policy in contemporary Britain seems to find its origins in American thinking and practice that the account which follows aims both to cast some light on the origins of pre-trial services in England and Wales and to suggest some ways in which trends in this area may develop in the future.

The concept of pre-trial release is inherent in the history of criminal justice. This can be traced back to the English Bill of Rights in 1689, which exhorted judges to issue a summons instead of a warrant for arrest, subsequent to the commission of an offence, if the judge was satisfied that the person summonsed would appear in court (Galvin and Busher 1977). It was not in Britain but in the United States, however, that pre-trial services first emerged, not just as a matter for judges and the courts, but as a matter of criminal justice administration and practice.

Pre-trial services: the beginnings

The history of bail and its reform in the United States dates back to the 1600s (see generally, Tobolowsky and Quinn 1993), but the non-discriminatory use of bail and pre-trial release did not emerge as a public issue until the 1950s (Bynum 1977), and the use of non-monetary pre-trial release did not become an issue until the 1960s (Clark and Boyd 1986).

---

[3] The work necessary to complete this review was generously supported by the chancellor and Department of Criminal Justice, University of Wisconsin Platteville.

In the early 1960s there was a growing concern about bail decision-making in the US courts. These concerns, which continued to grow, were centred on the evidence that the financially based and offence-orientated administration of bail inevitably led to the unnecessary pre-trial detention of defendants throughout both federal and state criminal justice systems. These concerns were galvanized into action and led to what one authority has called an unprecedented decade of bail reform (Tobolowsky and Quinn 1993).

This action was first manifest in 1961 when the Vera Foundation (later the Vera Institute) initiated the Manhattan Bail Project, with the simple objective of increasing the use of pre-trial release without the imposition of financial conditions (see Ares 1963). The Vera Foundation was established by a grant from an industrialist (Louis Schweitzer) who, after observing the conditions in one of New York's gaols, endowed the foundation to assist defendants too poor to afford their own financial surety for bail. The project was based on the belief that more defendants could be released pre-trial, without financial surety, and would be of good behaviour, if the court could be confidently informed about the defendant's stability and community ties. To accomplish its goal, staff in the project interviewed defendants on their first appearance in court to gather information about their family and community ties, employment, criminal history and current charges. Following attempts to verify the information, project staff then made an assessment of whether a non-financial release recommendation to the judge was appropriate.

The Manhattan Bail Project was remarkably successful. In its first year or so of operation, the courts granted bail to 60 per cent of those defendants where the project made a positive recommendation, compared to 14 per cent of a control group. Of the 250 defendants granted bail as a result of a positive recommendation by the project, only three failed to present themselves at court and only two were rearrested for fresh offences. Furthermore, the project had a number of positive unintended or unanticipated consequences. A significantly higher percentage of the bailed group than the control group (60 per cent versus 23 per cent) were acquitted or had their charges withdrawn, and a significantly lower percentage of the bailed group than the control group (21 per cent versus 96 per cent) were sentenced to prison (Ares 1963; Tobolowsky and Quinn 1993).

A decade of reform

The success of the Manhattan Bail Project led to it becoming a model of bail reform efforts throughout the United States. In 1963 four other jurisdictions had established bail projects, and over fifty were in existence by 1965 (Tobolowsky and Quinn 1993).

The impetus for the development of formal pre-trial release programmes was initiated by two national conferences, in 1964 and 1965. In 1966 the legal right to pre-trial release was enshrined in the Bail Reform Act 1966 (the first major reform of federal bail policy since the Judiciary Act 1789). The Act was intended to ensure that, regardless of financial status, no person should be needlessly detained when such detention does not serve the interests of justice or the public. Furthermore, Congress at this time suggested that if restriction was necessary to ensure a defendant's appearance at court, then the least amount of restriction necessary should be applied. In this way, the 1966 Act went beyond the concept and objectives of the Manhattan Bail Project actually to require that bail be granted (in non-capital cases), on personal recognizance or unsecured bond, unless the court considers that release under these conditions will not reasonably assure that the defendant duly appears at the appointed court.

Although the Bail Reform Act 1966 applied only to the federal courts, it was significant in two further ways. Firstly, the Act extended the factors courts must take into account in determining bail and the likelihood of assuring attendance at a future court date from the traditional (seriousness, nature and circumstances of the offence, the evidence, and previous convictions), to include additional factors concerning the defendant's stability and community ties. Secondly, it acted as a stimulus to the development of pre-trial services throughout the country at non-federal court levels. There are insufficient comprehensive national statistics on the growth of local programmes to gauge the level of development fully. However, by the end of this first decade there were over 100 local pre-trial projects in existence. Many of these projects were based on the 'own recognisance' model, but increasingly projects sought to exploit the expanded conditions concerning the granting of bail, and throughout the 1970s and 1980s the number of projects which made use of these conditions continued to grow (Tobolowsky and Quinn 1993).

At the federal level, pre-trial services began as demonstration projects in ten courts in 1975 (Hughes and Henkel 1997). These federal demonstration projects grew out of a growing number of local programmes, which were begun in the late 1960s and early 1970s. The local pre-trial programmes were often seen as advocacy projects – attempts to how many defendants could be released from jail. The federal programme, however, started from the position that pre-trial services were not about individual advocacy, but that they were provided as a service to the courts.

There was great enthusiasm for pre-trial services, in these early years, across the political, judicial and criminal justice spectrum. The Pretrial Services Act 1982 expanded the ten demonstration projects to all federal judicial districts, and put in place standards and procedures for the courts to follow in creating pre-trial services.

The Pretrial Services Act of 1982 mandates that the Director of the Administrative Office of the United States Courts under the supervision and direction of the Judicial Conference shall provide for the establishment of pretrial services in each judicial district other than the District of Columbia.

These pretrial services shall be administered by chief probation officers or, on recommendation of the district court with approval of the Circuit Judicial Council, by chief pretrial services officers who are not U.S. probation officers.

The primary pretrial services functions include investigating each defendant charged with an offense other than a petty offense, recommending appropriate release conditions, and supervising those persons released to pretrial services custody. (US Congress 1983)

Following an eighteen-month implementation period, after the passage of the 1982 Act, a senior representative of the judiciary, giving evidence to Congress, concluded that:

The judiciary endorses the pretrial services program. Our commitment is evident in the steps we have taken to implement it. If the Congress appropriates sufficient funding, I believe that with the orientation, training, and technical assistance provided to the district courts, and the cooperative efforts of the judiciary and supporting court personnel, it is reasonable to expect that the mandates of the legislation will be met successfully. (Tjoflat 1983)

Backlash

There were early signs, however, of a crack in the commitment to the concept of pre-trial services. Just two years later, in 1984, the Bail Reform Act enshrined the authorization of the use of pre-trial detention for more serious offenders. Although Congress indicated that the use of pre-trial detention was appropriate only under very limited circumstances, and although it did not seek to abandon or modify the objective of pre-trial services to reduce or avoid the unnecessary use of pre-trial detention, the Bail Reform Act indicates, perhaps, a very early weakening in the political enthusiasm for and commitment to pre-trial services.

Although, at the state level, pre-trial release programmes in the 1970s and 1980s were characterized by a maintenance of the achievements made in the 1960s and legislatures expanded opportunities for increased pre-trial release, there was also evidence of a 'backlash'. Prompted by increased public concerns about crime, legislatures also adopted measures which effectively restricted pre-trial release opportunities. Pre-trial legislation of the 1960s made assurances of future court appearances the sole criterion in determining pre-trial release conditions. In the 1970s and 1980s, however, assurances of public safety were added as an additional and equal criterion in determining bail conditions. More significantly, there was an increased enactment and extension of provisions authorizing preventive detention and the denial of any bail following an unfavourable risk assessment and determination of a defendant's 'dangerousness'.

On the one hand it is possible to see the growth in pre-trial services provision in the US during this period as a considerable achievement. On the other hand, the growth in the pre-trial detainee population (see below) and the limited coverage of pre-trial services paint a different picture. The rate of pre-trial detention in the early 1990s suggested that the costly imposition of pre-trial detention was not restricted to those defendants charged with more serious offences and those who posed the sort of danger to the community that Congress had in mind when it passed the Bail Reform Act of 1984 (Hughes 1993). Furthermore, in the year to September 1992, 54 per cent of defendants were held in detention at the point of sentencing, and 36 per cent of all federal pre-trial defendants remained in detention throughout their proceedings. By the mid-1980s the ambivalence concerning the pre-trial movement was evident. As one authority put it, 'Just as the federal Bail Reform Act of 1966 symbolized the culmination of the bail reform movement of the 1960s, the federal Bail Reform Act of 1984 symbolized the backlash against these reforms during the 1970s and 1980s' (Tobolowsky and Quinn 1993).

As noted previously, the 1984 Act retained the presumption in favour of bail, but it made bail conditional upon a determination that release would not endanger the safety of others. Where granted, bail was still to be based on the least restrictive conditions necessary to secure appearance at a future court date, but the 1984 Act expanded the factors to be considered in determining bail conditions in a way which increased those related to increased risks. While these reforms sparked a continuing debate over the wisdom and constitutionality of preventive detention and assessments of risk, the culmination of a period of thirty years of reform resulted in a situation in which courts had a wide range of options in attaching conditions to bail, and at the same time a variety of mechanisms to assure a defendant's detention.

The need for pre-trial services

Anyone even remotely familiar with the American experience of crime and criminal justice over recent years will have some idea of the need for pre-trial services. It is interesting that although the pre-trial literature avers suggestions of a massive increase in crime, one conclusion is universal: 'Skyrocketing incarceration rates have become a defining characteristic of America's criminal justice system' (Meyer and Holloway 1993).

Optimism in the American criminological literature is rarely found, as academics and official publications evince pessimism over the growing prison population. Between 1981 and 1992, for example, the federal pre-trial detention system experienced a fourfold increase in the average daily pre-trial detention population, from 5,000 to 20,000; with a concurrent projection of a further doubling in four years (Hughes 1993). From 1960 to 1995 the incarceration rate per 100,000 population increased sixfold in the United States (Buddress 1997). These increases have occurred, contrary to what one might have expected, despite the growth of pre-trial services and sustained growth in the number of staff employed in this activity (Hughes and Henkel 1997). How has this situation come about? As we shall see, the answer is not wholly to be found in the political backlash against the so-called liberalism of the 1960s and the Reaganite policies of being tough on crime – although these did play their part.

'Just deserts' and managerialism

It is well recognized that the 1970s witnessed a growing amount of scepticism concerning the efficacy of rehabilitation and the associated indeterminacy of sentencing. The swing away from rehabilitation to 'just deserts' as a sentencing philosophy was becoming established:

> But few could have foreseen the sweeping changes brought about by the enactment of the Comprehensive Crime Control Act of 1984. The virtual replacement of rehabilitation by a 'just deserts' model and the phasing out of parole marked a definitive end to an era which began with such optimism for the ideals of 'human reclamation'. Now, sentencing guidelines and mandatory minimum sentences set the tone and the probation officer-as-caseworker role no longer predominates. While the pendulum yet may swing back from crime control to individualized treatment, the system has undergone a profound transformation. The repercussions of it may be with us for years to come. (Hughes and Henkel 1997)

In the 1970s and early 1980s, several national studies (Wice 1972; Toborg 1982; Thomas 1976; Pryor and Smith 1982) demonstrated the effectiveness of pre-trial programmes as alternatives to custody. These evaluations consistently showed that pre-trial programmes have not endangered victims or the community, and they have minimized non-appearance rates. Despite growths in staffing and workload, the early promise of pre-trial services has failed to make a significant impact on the ever increasing prison population in the United States. An important clue to the dynamics which have brought this situation about is to be found in the collection of articles, published in the journal *Federal Probation* in 1993, in which many of the authors make a self proclaimed 'call to arms' in support of human-centred criminal justice and pre-trial services in opposition to what many saw as the draconian response to crime over the preceding decade (Broderick 1993).

The impact of these so-called draconian criminal justice policies was quite dramatic. Incarceration rates in the United States remained fairly stable, at about 100 per 100,000, from the late 1800s to the end of the 1970s. In the 1980s, however, and following the change in policy and philosophy enshrined in the Comprehensive Crime Control Act 1984, the incarceration rate rocketed to 600 per 100,000 population by the mid-1990s (Buddress 1997). What brought about this dramatic change in incarceration rates? The political 'get tough' on crime rhetoric may have been a contributory factor, so too may have been increasing public awareness of the 'drug problem' and the associated detection strategies of the police (Visher 1992), but more importantly we must look to the central features of the draconian policies to find an answer.

The draconian criminal justice policies of the United States from the mid-1980s onwards are characterized by two features: a 'just deserts' sentencing system and an increasingly pervasive managerialism. To be sure there is nothing inherent in a just deserts philosophy in itself that automatically leads to increased rates of incarceration. The key to 'just deserts' and an increase in incarceration lies in the detail of the model. It is in this detail, in the United States of the mid-1980s, that we find the introduction and expansion of mandatory minimum sentencing and, as far as pre-trial decision-making was concerned, increasing restrictions on the discretion of the judiciary to grant bail. Thus, from the mid-1980s the tightening of the criteria on which bail may be granted and the expansion of criteria for which bail may not be granted increased.

Of themselves, however, this particular manifestation of 'just deserts', even when backed by political 'get tough' policies, cannot explain the totality of the changes in incarceration rates. To complete the answer, it is necessary to understand the impact of 'managerialism' on criminal justice practice in the United States.

In the criminal justice sphere, managerialism may be understood as the introduction of administrative and technological tools into decision-making and practice activities. With particular reference to pre-trial services, managerialism was manifest in three main areas: judicial decision-making, the organization of services and control technologies.

In respect of judicial decision-making managerialism was most pervasive in the form of 'risk assessments'. First introduced in the mid-1980s, risk assessment became an integral part of the bail decision. Although risk assessments were initially based upon the skill and professionalism of probation and pre-trial officers, they were rapidly transformed into standardized risk assessment tools in which the officers (and the judges) had little discretion. These standardized risk assessment tools were, however, malleable in the hands of policy-makers and susceptible to political manipulation and the increasing definition of what constituted 'risk'.

As far as the organization of services was concerned, pre-trial services in the United States not only burgeoned, they became absorbed into the system – as an integral part of a complex criminal justice process. This absorption not only meant that pre-trial services took on the dominant philosophy of the criminal justice system (rather than espousing and practising its own 'humanitarian' ideal), but it meant that the organization of pre-trial services took the shape of the changing organization of criminal justice. Increasing specialization within criminal justice agencies reflected the needs of the system. As agencies grew in size they were increasingly organized into smaller specialized units as a managerial imperative. This trend was fed by the increasing complexity of individual tasks and the need for workers to limit their range of practice.

These changes were compounded by the introduction and growth in control technologies. These control technologies are firmly rooted in the managerialist tradition as a necessary response to several features of modern criminal justice systems: namely a desire to cut costs, increasing caseloads, and the associated need for those at the apex of central and local systems to control the amount and nature of professional activity – and to attempt to gain control over system behaviour and throughput. In practice these control technologies were both administrative and 'technical' in nature. Risk assessment tools have already been mentioned in this regard, but equally important for the character of pre-trial programmes was the introduction and expansion of conditions attached to bail. Early bail practices were characterized essentially by just one condition: to turn up at court. Increasingly, however, additional conditions were invented and applied, following the philosophy and practices of risk assessment. Many such conditions were administrative in character (for example curfew, reporting restrictions and refraining conditions), such as may be breached by overt behaviour. Increasingly, however, technology has pervaded this area as electronic monitoring (Renzema and Skelton 1991) and compulsory drug testing (Carver 1993) technologies became available – alongside the growth and availability of information technologies (Cadigan 1993).

These control technologies tighten the net of control around individuals, they make a breach of bail conditions more amenable to detection and they make compliance more difficult as those granted bail must continually submit themselves to scrutiny. Simultaneously, these control technologies reduce the discretion of criminal justice professionals who are exposed to increasingly tightly defined codes of practice and simple 'yes' or 'no' measures of compliance. The impact of such measures obviously leads to high rates of technical breach of bail conditions and return to prison – at a rate of over 80 per cent in California (Buddress 1997).

Taken together, therefore, the twin processes of just deserts and managerialism have operated to nullify and swamp the potential contribution of pre-trial services to reducing the prison population in the United States. As one author has rather pessimistically stated,

> The pretrial diversion movement was spawned in the wake of 1960s reforms and represented a major departure from current criminological practice. The thinking was that diversion would shift the focus from a punitive orientation to a client-centred or 'helping' approach. Simultaneously, diversion offered a panacea to the system's aging aches and pains. In the final analysis, the diversion movement has not achieved many (if any) of the reforms or goals that were originally formulated. Its survival today is based almost exclusively in terms of how well it serves the political interests of the jurisdiction in which it is located. Helping the offender is no longer what the diversion movement is all about. (Matthews 1998)

This chapter has reviewed the origins and history of pre-trial services in the United Kingdom and the United States of America. A number of common themes emerge – the crisis of carceral policies, the vitality of the intellectual case for pre-trial services, contrasted with their marginalization in actual practice.

The chapter which follows aims to burrow below the broad sweep and the headline messages of the scene-setting attempted here. By looking in detail at contemporary practice, it aims to discover the best of pre-trial work in the Probation Service in England and Wales and to learn the lessons of that experience.

3. Models of Good Practice

Introduction

In presenting a case for the adoption of pre-trial work this chapter attempts to answer two central questions: what is best practice to date and what can we learn from it? This chapter's arguments are based on original research conducted between September 1998 and December 1999 in a selected sample of three probation areas. The argument is presented in two ways. Firstly a descriptive element, with accompanying charts and statistical data, telling the individual story of what resources have been deployed, in what way and to what effect in the probation services visited. Secondly, and more importantly, the chapter discusses these findings in themes to draw out points of similarity and difference, but more essentially to focus on what can be learnt from these services that might be used elsewhere. For those unfamiliar with pre-trial work the first part of this chapter together with the descriptions of the work in chapter 2 may be useful. For those with some knowledge and less time the thematic discussion which follows is intended to stand by itself as a summary and discussion of the essential findings and possible implications for policy and practice.

Description of project and methodology

Selection of the research sample

The three probation areas studied were selected from those few areas identified during phase one of this project as having a substantial and continuing involvement in pre-trial service work in addition to bail information (Haines and Octigan 1999). They were also chosen because they represent between them a mix of large metropolitan areas, urban areas and rural areas, and offer an insight into the particular needs and problems of these locations.

They are intended as a useful comparison for other services in similar areas. Particular attention is focused on the strengths and weaknesses of the type of services provided in the study areas and their methods and models of service provision. All three probation areas in this study had bail information and bail support schemes which originated during or before the period of hypothecated funding and have since run with the continuing, though in two areas diminished, support of their services.

In assessing pre-trial services this study concentrates on bail information, bail support and some work of hostels with those clients. It also looks at partnership arrangements that were responsible for the delivery of the majority of bail support schemes. Space and time have excluded any extensive discussion of related pre-trial work such as mentally disordered offender diversion schemes, public-interest case assessment and cautioning and diversion strategies for young offenders. The purpose of this study has been to look at pre-trial work for young and adult defendants that could form part of a universal and mainstream probation service to the courts.

Research method

The research conducted in these three selected probation areas had three clear elements:

(a) A schedule of visits and interviews to establish the scope and purpose of all the relevant sites of operation including bail support, bail information schemes and hostels. This also included partnership-run schemes and, for comparison, one project for mentally disordered offenders.

(b) Interviews with a sample of key people within the local criminal justice system with an interest in and contribution to the pre-trial process including sentencers, clerks, prosecutors, solicitors and defendants. These were selected and arranged by managers from the probation service in the area visited. Interviews were scheduled to last one hour each, and questions focused on interviewees' knowledge of and evaluation of pre-trial services within their petty sessional division (see Appendix for questions and schedule of visits).

(c) An examination of all available data, documents and evaluations of pre-trial work kept or commissioned by the three services.

The aim of the research was to explore the various types of pre-trial work being undertaken and to draw from these elements a model of good practice that might be of value to other probation services. Interviewees were aware of the aims of the project and asked to comment freely on their experiences of the process and to offer their observations and evidence of the strengths and weaknesses of their scheme. The identity of interviewees and that of the service areas visited has been kept from this evaluation to allow a frank discussion of the issues raised. Some comments and data are therefore quoted without reference to their source.

The study had certain limitations. There was only time to visit each area for a maximum of five days, although these were efficiently timetabled to maximize use of time. The interview schedules were organized on request by managers within the services, and must therefore represent a sample of services that reflect practice that they were confident to show. In particular, they may not be representative where only two or three examples of hostels or bail information schemes could be visited out of a total of seven or eleven respectively.

There was also a lack of detailed evaluative material in two of the three areas, which limited any detailed quantitative assessment of the services. Those studies available were used, but to preserve anonymity are not referenced in the bibliography.

It became clear during the research that prison bail information teams play a significant role in the pre-trial process, but there was no opportunity to visit and evaluate these separately. That could effectively form the basis of a further study of pre-trial work.

Description of the three probation areas visited

Area 1
Geography
This was a predominantly rural area with several small areas of urban concentration. The possibility for pre-trial work was made more difficult by the need to cover the work of a number of small magistrates' courts, which tried an average of fewer than ten defendants with bail issues per day. The advantage was, however that a smaller number of sentencers, clerks and prosecutors were involved and their support and views more easily canvassed. The area had

four prisons, one probation hostel and one voluntary hostel. These served three Crown Courts and four petty sessional divisions.

Funding

Funding for pre-trial work was limited to the probation budget. Although bids had been made to the Single Regeneration Budget and for European funding they were unsuccessful. This was attributed to the time taken to put forward a competitive bid and to the areas' low priority. Funding had continued to be made through probation partnership money, but the lack of a key performance indicator for pre-trial work was putting this funding under threat. The service had been reduced in the year before the visit, and the probation committee had withheld £10,000 of the fund of £50,000 paid to the partner per year for reconsideration.

Range of pre-trial work

This service had a bail information officer in each court every morning to identify and supply information to the court via prosecutors for all those identified as at risk of remand in custody. They were part of the court team and shared these duties with other court duties. There was no cover in the afternoon and occasional cases were necessarily missed. The service employs probation service assistants to undertake its bail information work in each court.

A Home Office-funded hostel provided bail beds and support to residents, including training/employment, group work and individual supervision. Defendants on bail also received support services from hostel staff in addition to the curfew and residence order imposed by the court.

A bail support scheme was run through a voluntary sector partner for under-25-year-olds identified by bail information officers at court as at risk of a remand in custody. The bail support package was part of a court bail order and supported by the police who had an arrangement to respond to notified breaches of reporting, residence or curfew conditions. The package included support with accommodation (sometimes in the bail hostel), employment/training and compulsory reporting and supervision. This partnership drew particularly on previous and current relations with a voluntary-sector partner and developing relations with statutory partners, particularly social services and police.

The prisons have bail information teams but commitment to them by the prisons was reportedly strong in one case and indifferent in the other.

Management structure and connections within Probation Service

An Assistant Chief Probation Officer (ACPO) held overall responsibility for pre-trial services under a general remit for partnerships and special services development. The ACPO also had line management responsibility for the bail support contract and work in the hostels. Court work, which included bail information, was the responsibility of another ACPO. A Senior Probation Officer (SPO) held a remit for enhancing quality and effectiveness, which included all pre-trial work, but with no line management responsibility for the staff actually doing the work.

Referral routes and second-time remand decisions
All defendants in the cells were potential targets for bail information and bail support. Bail information officers made decisions on whom to refer for bail support and, although the partner agency could refuse a referral, in practice they were contracted to accept and work with whoever was sent. Breach decisions were the responsibility of the bail support provider, but then passed to the Probation Service court team for enforcement.

Prison bail information officers at one prison saw second-time remands, but not at the other where a scheme had not been maintained. There was no clear system for the transfer of information about defendants between prison and court.

Assessment and evaluation material and systems
The service's bail support scheme had been evaluated by a consultant and by NACRO in the two years before the visit. These reports were made available and provided an insight into the workings of the scheme. However, neither these reports nor the service kept any substantial quantitative or qualitative data on the pre-trial work. Information was available on the number of bail information reports presented and the outcome of the bail decisions. There was no systematic evaluation of the content of the reports or correlation with offence, nor any information on the quality and success of bail support other than numbers of orders started and completed or breached.

Partnership and contract

The partner was a voluntary charitable organization operating locally with a number of contracts for work with the local authority, police and social services. It specialized in work with young people with a variety of social problems, including criminal behaviour. The staff were recruited without qualifications but many had teaching or social work backgrounds. They received induction and in-house training and were able to attend occasional days of Probation Service training where relevant. This focused on drug awareness and counselling skills.

The contract for bail support work was per client and renewed annually. The referrals all came from bail information workers at court. The contract had no stipulations or detail about the work expected other than that clients would be supervised and breached for non-compliance. These terms were not defined or quantified.

The partner had no staff dedicated to the bail support work but allocated cases to its full- and part-time staff, who also worked with other young people through other contract work.

Pre-trial service provision in probation area 1

Probation area

4 prisons
1 probation and one voluntary hostel
3 Crown Courts and
4 petty sessional divisions

Probation Service staff

ACPO: responsibility for pre-trial work and other specialisms including prisons and hostels
SPO: some input from quality and effectiveness SPO
Probation Service officers: 5 part-time on bail information

Partnership staff

Partnership manager as co-ordinator and manager of pre-trial bail support work
Pool of up to 25 duty staff to supervise bail support on 24-hour rota basis.

Funding: probation budget

Partnership money: up to £50,000 per annum paid incrementally on completion of bail support orders

Area 2

Geography

A large, concentrated metropolitan area with a number of large areas of population clustered around a major inner city area. The area has the advantage of economies of scale in providing services to its courts but must also overcome the challenges of greater economic and social deprivation. The area has three Crown Courts, fifteen petty sessional divisions, three prisons and seven hostels.

Funding

As in area 1, pre-trial work was sustained from probation budget core funding, and bail support work through partnership money. No external funding had been applied for or used. Partnership projects were funded partly by probation but in collaboration with social services in one case, social services and health in another, and a national voluntary charity in the third.

Range of pre-trial work

Bail information schemes offer bail information to the court via the prosecutor on all offenders in target categories (under-21-year-olds, women, people from ethnic minorities and those deemed vulnerable, especially the mentally ill). The service employs Probation Service assistants to undertake its bail information work in each court. Bail support packages are offered both to young offenders (under twenty-one) through partnerships with voluntary-sector providers and in partnership with health and social services to mentally disordered offenders. Seven Home Office-funded hostels provided bail beds and support to residents including training/employment, group work and individual supervision.

Two bail support schemes offered bail support to under-21-year-old defendants bailed by magistrates. A joint funded partnership between Health Trust, probation and social services offers support and intervention for mentally disordered offenders at all stages of court process, including bail information and bail support.

Management structure and connections within the probation service

As in area 1, the management of pre-trial work was shared between ACPOs. One oversaw special projects including the hostels and bail support, whilst another was responsible for court work and bail information. An SPO with responsibility for quality and effectiveness also had responsibility for the quality of pre-trial work. One court SPO was critical of this structure because competing priorities within the court service marginalized bail information work.

Referral routes

As in area 1, the referral system for pre-trial work centred on the work of the bail information officers who assessed defendants for both bail information reports and bail support. Defendants were referred on first or second appearance for bail information or bail support.

Assessment and evaluation material and systems

Data evaluating bail support and bail information services were not readily available. Statistical data were kept at the services' headquarters, collected on standardized case assessment forms across a range of probation tasks. From this it was possible to isolate information about the quantity of bail support supervisions and bail information reports undertaken, but no clear information existed on quality and performance. One partner organization had produced a report on success rates for its bail support programme and this has been quoted in this report.

Partnership

As noted above, four partners were involved in the three pre-trial bail support projects run for this Probation Service – health, social services and two national children's charities. The contracts were, as in area 1, an arrangement of payment based on numbers of clients worked with. Clear targets on assessment of quality or detailed definitions of the work entailed were not included.

Pre-trial service provision in probation area 2
3 Crown Courts
15 petty sessional divisions
3 prisons
7 hostels.
Probation Service staff.
ACPO: responsibility for pre-trial work and other specialisms
SPO: some input from court SPO
Probation officers: one full time mental health diversion scheme.

Hostels: seven
Probation Service officers: each court

Team assistant staff
Partnership staff
Two partnership-funded young offender bail support schemes (17–25)

Funding
Partnership money for bail support in three-way arrangement with
voluntary sector partners and social services. Paid per client.
Mental health diversion scheme:
Seconded probation officer, shared resources with community health and
hospital-based psychiatrist.

Area 3
Geography
A large, sprawling metropolitan area which had a number of centres
of population and rural boundaries. There were areas in which
economies of scale were possible but wider co-ordination across a
number of urban areas was necessary. The area had three Crown
Courts, eleven petty sessional divisions, two prisons and eight hostels.

Funding
Core funding was used to employ Probation Service assistants and
probation officers to undertake bail information as well as bail
support work. This included a full-time SPO and PO to oversee the
work of the bail information officers and the work of the bail
support officers. This was a significant reduction in staffing from
two and three years before, yet still represented a significant
commitment to pre-trial work above that found in areas 1 and 2.

Two voluntary-sector providers undertook the bail support
work, with the Probation Service providing all of the funding
through partnership money. This had been supplemented by
significant funding from a successful Single Regeneration Budget
bid for £40,000, half of which was being allocated to a new bail
support drugs initiative.

Range of pre-trial work
A bail information officer worked in each court offering bail
information to the court for targeted defendants. Bail support

packages including accommodation, supervision and training were supplied by voluntary-sector partner agencies to under-25-year-old defendants bailed by the magistrates' court across the probation area in one case, and in one suburban area in the other. There were bail information schemes at both prisons.

One hundred and twenty defendants received bail support during 1998, and bail information reports were provided for 250 bail supportees. Seven hostels provided a range of services for bailees including drug counselling, group work, supervision and accommodation.

Referral procedures

For bail information reports this area targeted all those defendants in the cells who were under twenty-five, female or from ethnic minorities. Unlike areas 1 and 2, bail support was offered only to defendants who had already been remanded in custody by magistrates (second-time remands).

Referral to bail hostels was facilitated by the use of a central bail referral officer who was responsible for finding and allocating defendants to bail hostels rather than leaving this to bail information officers or hostel staff as in other probation areas.

Management structure and connections within the probation service

The role of the ACPO responsible for pre-trial work was more clearly aligned with the work of the pre-trial team, although court work was still the responsibility of another ACPO. However, as noted, this service had appointed a full-time SPO and a full-time PO to oversee all pre-trial work, responsible to the ACPO, and their work had resolved many of the problems of accountability and communication reported by the other two areas.

Assessment, evaluation and systems

The co-ordination of services within the line management structure, and the focus given by a full time SPO and PO, had produced a much clearer set of targets and procedures for monitoring and improving the work than was apparent in the other two areas. Annual reports assessed the work of pre-trial services (excluding the hostels) and demonstrated its effectiveness.

Partnership

The scheme visited was run by NACRO and provided bail support to the entire probation area. One supervisor and two part-time bail support officers supervised all of the 100 or so bail support packages each year).

Pre-trial service provision in probation area 3.

Probation area

3 Crown Courts
11 petty sessional divisions
2 prisons
8 hostels.

Probation Service staff

ACPO: responsibility for pre-trial services, hostels and sex offenders
SPO: full-time pre-trial services
Probation officers: two full-time
Probation Service officers: eight full-time, six part-time
Team assistant staff: three full-time

Partnership staff

Bail support: one full-time co-ordinator/bail support officer
Two part-time bail support officers
Second bail support scheme in one court area. Young offenders (17) only

Funding

Probation budget: £420,411 in 1999 (reduced from £683,406 in 1994)
Partnership money: £40,000 to partner on rolling renewable annual
  programme
Single Regeneration Budget: £20,000 towards drug bail initiative.

This concludes the section on information. What follows is a critical and themed discussion of the findings.

Discussion of evidence from the pre-trial services in the three areas

The findings of the research are discussed under four headings identifying those areas of pre-trial work that were examined in detail: bail information, bail support, partnership and hostels. These are interleaved by subheadings that provide a framework for an evaluation of them: management structure and funding, communication and organization, outcome and evaluation. All the sections include a summary box of strengths and weaknesses and five key points to identify the key findings and arguments. The points raised were all made during the research interviews and found to be significant, either by defining the work or as observations on particular strengths or weaknesses of the pre-trial work in question. As noted in the introduction to this chapter, if the reader needs a fuller description of what is meant by these terms it will be found in chapter 2. The details of the data and how they and these observations were collected are in the first part of the present chapter.

Pre-trial services 1: bail information

Management, structure and funding

Bail information officers, prosecutors and magistrates uniformly observed that bail information made a worthwhile contribution to the bail process. All the clerks and magistrates interviewed saw bail information as a helpful and worthwhile activity. As one magistrate put it, 'Bail decisions are important in maintaining a balance between the rights of the defendant and public risk. Any information that helps us to make that decision is useful.' Prosecutors were also positive about the value of the information given and expressed faith in the Probation Service for its reliability in supplying it. There was therefore a universal declaration of support for the idea of bail information schemes from within and without the probation service. Because of this commitment, funding from core budgets and KPI status since January 2000, the management commitment to supporting and funding bail information work in the three areas was strong. There were bail information schemes in all courts visited in the three areas (not always reflected nationally – see Haines and Octigan 1998) with dedicated and trained staff.

The disadvantage that bail information officers and court senior probation officers identified was a lack of clear routes of accountability connecting bail information work with the other pre-trial services, and a lack of connection with client supervision

---

Bail information schemes: five key points

- Court favour. Court staff, prosecutors and magistrates universally welcomed bail information as providing a positive contribution to safe and fair bail decisions.
- Best value. The comprehensive spending review estimated that bail information could save £9 million on remand costs, and a further £18 million with investment in hostel places (see chapter 4).
- Room for improvement. Poor communication between court and prison bail teams on incomplete or unsuccessful bail information work means that progress at each stage can be lost. There is potential for greater effectiveness through better communication and co-ordination between remands.
- Poor relation. Bail information work is reportedly marginalized by probation and court services and is not reaching its potential through lack of time, consideration and resources.
- Future moves. The potential for swift, full and accurate bail information through computerized case and criminal records is vast. As yet, practice in recording, sharing and standardizing this information is reportedly patchy, both within probation and across the criminal justice system.

---

teams. Bail information officers reported a lack of guidelines and training, and greater priority given to other court duties, which tended to reduce time given to bail information work. This was particularly so in areas 1 and 2, but in area 3 the bail information officers reported directly to the pre-trial PO, and through him to an SPO with no competing priorities outside pre-trial work. This apparently avoided the problems of marginalization seen in the other two areas.

Despite support from managers and staff these areas did not, however, guarantee to provide a service to all defendants, nor were there bail information services in two of the ten prisons in the three areas. For the prisons the relevant ACPOs considered it to be a question of competing priorities. In the rural courts represented in the study (four out of six in area 1) and in two of the smaller courts in area 2, the provision of bail information in the afternoon sessions was judged by the ACPO and SPO respectively not to be cost-effective. This was due to very small numbers of defendants passing through after 2 p.m., and the need for bail information officers to attend to other duties in the afternoon. For the most part, however, there was a commitment to bail information for all defendants in targeted groups.

Communication and organization
Targeting of defendants to choose those most likely to be at risk of a remand in custody
Bail information officers in all three areas used pre-selected criteria to target defendants at greater risk of custody. In defining these priority groups, all three services included the categories of ethnic minorities, women and young offenders (under twenty-one or under twenty-five), and anybody else considered vulnerable, especially the mentally disordered. It was not possible to evaluate the outcome of this policy because neither the Probation Service (except in area 3) nor the courts (see chapter 4) kept information on the outcome of bail information decisions. In effect, prioritizing was necessary only when the bail information officer had less time than was needed to see all defendants. In smaller courts this was seldom a problem, but in larger courts it was commonly the case.

The bail information officers interviewed all described using their professional judgement about whom to target. This was based on information from police and prosecutors on defendants for whom there was an opposition to bail, and by using experience in assessing the known factors – usually previous record, seriousness of offence and personal circumstances. Two officers were new to the job and described having to learn as they went in the absence of precise information. There was a consensus of opinion that this area of work could benefit from more systematic evaluation and training.

Time before court was also held by bail information officers to be too short to perform their work thoroughly
Because of the busy timetables which courts keep, and the number of defendants produced each day, bail information officers were often unable to interview all defendants before their hearings. In smaller courts it was possible for bail information officers to see up to twelve defendants in a morning, but it was not seen as cost-effective by managers for them to remain in the afternoon when few defendants were produced, if any. In larger courts up to fifty defendants came through per day, and it was impossible to see all

of them in the time between their arrival (9 a.m.) and the court sitting (10 a.m.).

Should information go to prosecutors?

Three bail information officers questioned the need to supply information only to prosecutors. They saw their job as lobbying prosecutors to divert them from opposing bail if positive information could achieve that. They would also, however, prefer in many cases to supply information to the court directly as happens with pre-sentence reports. In some courts it was standard practice only to supply bail information to prosecutors, as the rules require. In others reports were given to the clerk and bench, and in some they were also either given to or asked for by defence solicitors. In addition, some bail, information officers spoke to or lobbied prosecutors before court about their opposition to bail whilst others had no direct contact with them at all. One magistrate expressed strong views on this process, arguing: 'It is for the bench to decide on bail and so we should have all available information to make that decision.'

There was clearly a need for more clarification and consistency on these issues. Giving bail information only to prosecutors meant in some reported cases that it was not used in court at all because the prosecutor chose not to. The magistrates were not therefore made aware of the information available at all even though it may have aided their decision-making.

Whether or not the court should receive full information

Bail information officers had previously supplied positive information only about defendants to the court. For example, bail information officers might withhold information that they received about a defendant's failed supervision history or drug addiction. This practice was much criticized by magistrates and prosecutors who all said that bail decisions needed to be made on 'full information' in order to take proper account of any risk to the public. In fact the Home Office has already taken on this point and the positive information rule was dropped in the national standards draft of January 2000. This required bail information reports to address a number of factors in the defendant's life by supplying full and verified information, positive and negative. This will now need to be researched further since it became required practice during the current research programme. The fear expressed by some managers that the supply of full information would affect the success of bail information in diverting defendants from custody may prove unfounded. As a Home Office circular puts it,

> The existence of bail information schemes does not necessarily reduce the likelihood of a defendant being remanded in custody. In some cases the scheme may identify risk factors which make a remand more likely. That is right: the public must be protected from those who are a genuine danger. But the overall impact of bail information has (in any case) been shown to reduce the number of defendants remanded in custody. (Home Office draft circular, 1/00)

Communication

Bail information is by its nature primarily concerned with information collection and communication systems. It relies on fast, accurate and verifiable information for its success. The systems that it relies on and uses are therefore crucial and those who participated in the study said much on this point. This included comments on intra-agency as well as inter-agency communication, and about issues of co-operation as much as about protocols and systems.

What information is supplied?

Bail information officers reported that they sought information primarily about address, offending history and any record of supervision. Both in this study and in previous studies of bail information (see Lloyd 1992; Burrows et al. 1994) it is apparent that practice currently varies from court to court depending largely on that developed by individual bail information officers. Only one factor was consistently supplied in the twenty reports examined in two of the researched areas — a verified address. This is in accordance not only with the chief factor in denying bail but also with the main fears of magistrates. As one magistrate put it, 'Our greatest fear is that defendants won't come back. A verified address goes a long way to satisfying that fear.'

In other respects the supply of information was not systematic, however, and more research needs to be done into the type of information effective with prosecutors and magistrates.

Retrieving and verifying information

The availability of records was crucial to the reliability and thoroughness of the scheme, but in most cases bail information officers reported that in reality access was always very patchy. Sometimes, and particularly after privatization of the cell security system in 1998, police records were not available in the cells at the time of interview. This lack has been addressed by some custody operators recently, and in most cases records are now reported to be reliably available. Access to previous convictions relies on the co-operation of the CPS, but this was also reportedly unreliable in all three areas. In fact two sentencers also raised the issue of the unreliability of the CPS in providing information on previous convictions to the court.

Access to probation records was also unreliable. Within the probation service the advent of Client Record Administration and Management System and other computerised record systems should have made the task of the bail information officer much easier in accessing offender supervision histories, current charges and previous convictions. Unfortunately the practice of probation officers in completing records reliably was not good according to several bail information officers, an SPO and an ACPO. Despite the potential usefulness of these systems they do not yet appear to be used effectively.

The timely completion of records was improving, however, according to some practitioners and managers. Several suggested that, because bail information work is not yet valued elsewhere in the Probation Service, probation officers do not see the value of keeping their case supervision notes up to date. In either case, the success of bail information clearly relies on speedy access to relevant and verified information. Transfer of information between court and prison bail information schemes was much criticized by practitioners, leading to lost opportunities and duplicated work.

There was in most cases a gap in communication between court and prison that undermined the potential for effective remand management at this stage. In one area use of faxes to send information was prohibited because it was seen as 'unsafe'. There were no standard procedures for supplying information to the prison bail information team about work undertaken at court – for example work in progress such as contacts remaining to be made or information yet to be verified. In some cases this information was passed to the relevant prison but two thirds of the bail information said that it was their experience that it was not acted on. Their experience was that prison officers would only offer bail information if an inmate asked to see them, and would not actively seek out potential bailees. This led to opportunities for information in favour of bail being lost in a number of cases, or work already undertaken being needlessly duplicated in others.

Again, because this study did not visit the prison bail information teams, there is scope for more research in this area.

Availability of recorded information

Additional information (beyond verification of address) sought by bail information officers owed more to the availability of records than to a systematic search for specific information. Most bail information searches were based on the availability of an up-to-date list of previous convictions, probation records on any kind of supervision or previous contact, and telephone conversations with hostel or probation staff who may have supervised the defendant in any capacity. Officers also relied on the availability of police and CPS papers to ascertain details of the seriousness of the charges and what objections to bail had or would be raised, to see how to answer those objections by the supply of information. Bail information officers reported that in none of these cases was the information reliably available, undermining the effectiveness of the scheme. This was clearly a matter for better co-operation and efficiency between these various parts of the criminal justice system.

In area 1 an attempt had been made to share access to computerized information on defendants between police and probation. The different technology of the systems and cost of access was proving to be a problem, but the in-principle agreement was felt to be a promising first step. It also signalled an agreement between the two agencies that responsibility for some aspects of bail management could and should be shared.

In area 2 communication between sections of the service was also reported to be difficult, particularly between bail information officers in court and prison, and between community supervision teams and hostels. There were no systems for ensuring that information about clients was available for bail information officers preparing reports to the court.

In all three areas there was no clear system for communicating information between prison and court bail information officers. A computerized probation record system had not been fully implemented in two of the three areas. The partner agency and two bail information officers said that easier access to client records would improve the effectiveness of their pre-trial work.

Outcome and evaluation

In research terms the records kept by the services visited were limited, and so a clear picture of how successful bail decisions based on bail information were could not be determined. There is a good case for conducting fuller research on a number of aspects of the bail information process, including the success or otherwise of targeting, the nature of the information supplied and the future conduct on bail of defendants bailed as a result of bail information reports.

Nevertheless, it is still worth including the statistical records that have been kept in these probation areas, which echo those referred to in more depth in the history chapter of this book. These identify clearly a number of key successes of bail information reports. In particular the number of reports produced, and the number of defendants successfully diverted into bail whose original application was opposed by the police, CPS or both. In one area the bail information statistics given in table 3.1 reveal this picture.

Table 3.1 Statistics on bail information (area 1, 1998–9)

Court areas covered	9
Bail information reports produced (first appearance)	2405
Court/prison bail information reports (subsequent appearance)	1830
Bail support packages provided	98
Bail information reports converted to bail	47%

Almost half of these reports resulted in bail being granted to the defendants. In the absence of complete information it is speculative, but if we assume, as policy dictates, that bail information reports are targeted at those for whom the CPS is asking for a remand in custody, this is a high level of success.

In another of the three areas figures have also been produced showing the success rate of bail information interventions in

Table 3.2 Success rate of bail information scheme (area 2, 1995–6)

Court areas covered	5
Defendants produced	1564
Defendants interviewed	430
Bail information reports produced	304
Defendants bailed	186
Defendants remanded in custody	118
Success rate	61%

converting requests for custody into bail (table 3.2). Here a 61 per cent success rate is found, which may reflect the more cautious targeting – about one-third of defendants interviewed, compared with nearly two-thirds in the area above.

However, although indicative of success within the system itself in persuading prosecutors and magistrates to choose in favour of bail where they were predicted not to, a fuller and more meaningful evaluation of bail information is needed. In particular there was little evidence of whether those decisions were the right ones in terms of accuracy, justice and protection of the public. Decisions were not followed through by probation or court to see whether the granting of bail had not led to the defendant absconding or committing further offences whilst on bail. Again, a fuller co-operation between court, probation and police could secure a more systematic approach to evaluating this work in the interests of making it more accurate, safe and cost-effective.

Within the areas researched only two sources of information on the quality of bail decisions were found – amongst hostel staff and sentencers.

Hostel view of bail information
The central bail referral officers in two areas and two hostel wardens in one area were particularly critical of the bail information process. In two areas it was pointed out that 40 per cent of those bailed to hostels on the assessment and recommendation of bail information officers failed to arrive (all are expected to arrive from court on the same day). Hostel staff in two hostels also complained that drug addicts in particular took trouble to mask their dependency when interviewed for bail and a problem became apparent only after arrival. Both problems they attributed to hasty and ill-researched

decisions by bail information staff. Bail information officers were themselves concerned at the lack of available information and the lack of time in which to collect or assess it. Those court staff who were interviewed were not aware of these problems.

Magistrates' view

One magistrate also made the point that when they suspect that probation staff are 'erring on the side of kindness', they place less weight on the information given anyway. This suggests that, with full information, courts may act more decisively when the available information is in support of bail. It is also arguable whether there is any reliable standard perception of what positive or negative information might be – like beauty, it may be in the eye of the beholder.

However, as stated above, the overall assessment of bail information work by sentencers and prosecutors was very positive, with a high degree of respect for the Probation Service as a provider of impartial, accurate and useful information.

Pre-trial services 2: bail support

All six of the bail support schemes visited during the research were funded in part, and in most cases in full, through probation

---

Bail support schemes: five key points
- Who's paying? Bail support is mostly funded through partnership money because it has no place in the KPI or formula funding as yet.
- Young offenders. Bail support currently targets young offenders under twenty-five and vulnerable adults. Some adults are included, but grant funding is more commonly targeted at vulnerable groups, including young people.
- On the bench. Magistrates support the scheme, but are not generally aware of the high level of supervision and 'escort to court' service that it offers.
- On the beat. Bail support worked with the support and co-operation of police in two of the three areas, with co-operation on the monitoring and enforcement of offending on bail.
- Proof of the pudding. Where records are kept, over two-thirds of those given bail support successfully completed their programme and returned to court.

partnership money. For this reason many of the issues which the research has raised are relevant to the issue of partnership, and to the service that was provided for the probation service by, in five cases, the voluntary sector. Examining the issue of partnership was therefore very significant in assessing these schemes. This section offers, first, an examination of the issues and comments made about bail support schemes that were separate from issues of its delivery within an inter-agency partnership. The section that follows examines the separate but related issues surrounding partnerships.

Management and policy issues

Bail support schemes operate across traditional organizational boundaries within the probation service in that they bring community supervision practice to what is a court probation setting. They also rely on hostel work, and some aspects of throughcare supervision are akin to the supervision of bailees in the community. It is therefore difficult to place the management of bail support work easily within the existing management structures of probation services or to locate it within traditional areas of expertise, particularly in the many services which have favoured specialized rather than generic work. Because, as noted, the work was also largely the responsibility of partner agencies it also fell within the remit of ACPOs responsible for partnership and community development.

This research project examined the work of six bail support schemes across the three probation areas. The general pattern was for a target client group (adults, mentally disordered defendants, people from ethnic minorities, women or young people) to be offered bail support via the court by a voluntary sector partner with expertise with that client group.

In two of the three areas investigated, three ACPOs had responsibility for different aspects of the work, particularly where it spanned court and community supervision work. By contrast in area 3 a single ACPO had responsibility, through a dedicated bail support SPO, for all pre-trial work, and this may be an explanation for the more successful targeting and communication systems in that area. In the other two areas a frequent criticism by bail staff was a lack of support for their work within the service with no single, clear management structure to identify or meet its needs or to respond effectively to difficulties.

Unlike areas 1 and 2, in area 3 bail support was offered only to defendants who had already been remanded in custody by magistrates (second-time remands). The rationale for this given by the ACPO and SPO was to prevent net-widening. Bail support was intended for those at risk of custody, and those already remanded were clearly at most risk of continuing to be remanded.

Operation of bail support schemes
The evidence on the operation of these schemes showed a variation in their delivery across and within the probation areas. This was not surprising given that schemes had generally developed from individual projects rather than from top-down management initiatives. Bail support schemes were, as noted, also managed and run by voluntary sector partner organizations with differing cultures, systems and priorities that created a variation in their operation. There were also few mechanisms for monitoring or evaluating the quality or detail of the work, and therefore few opportunities for applying a systematic approach to the work. This was also a consequence of there being no national standard for bail support work.

This is evident, for example, in assessing what constituted a bail support package for a defendant. The focus of the work varied from client to client in its scope and content. The number of supervision sessions varied, for example, between one and three per week, and those varied in length between one minute to two hours. The focus of the work was sometimes on personal and relationship problems, sometimes on employment and sometimes on offending issues. Breach for non-compliance varied between immediate breach for not showing for an appointment to breach for a series of missed appointments without explanation.

This could also be seen as a strength, of course, as two partner organizations argued. They believed in the effectiveness of building a good working relationship between bailee and supervisor based on respect and support. This arguably reflected the counselling background and voluntary nature of these service providers.

In this light it was more remarkable how similar the schemes were in the general pattern and system of their operation, as defined above and in the history chapter. In particular, all schemes undertook individual supervision of bailees, and in two schemes provided an escort to court to ensure compliance with bail conditions. In two areas regular liaison and co-operation with police over enforcement of bail were well established, and in all three a breach for non-compliance was responded to by a return to court, enforced by the probation service.

Communication and organization
For example, in one area there were no systems for including feedback on defendants undergoing bail support to probation officers preparing pre-sentence reports. A hostel manager also complained that hostel staff prepared detailed reports on bailees supervised by the hostel, which were not systematically referred to in pre-sentence reports.

Lack of information
Magistrates raised a common criticism that feedback and proper evaluation were either missing or not conveyed to them, which was seriously undermining their confidence in the schemes in their areas. As one probation committee chair put it, 'We need assurance of monitoring. Sentencers are persuaded by statistical evidence – and need more proof of the effectiveness of bail support. Defendants will agree to anything in order to be bailed – they may not actually be listening.'

Again, from another magistrate: 'The probation service needs to communicate the detail and purpose and success of pre-trial services to magistrates. They need to know. There is a huge credibility and information gap – many magistrates believe that probation officers do not keep to national standards.

Outcome and evaluation
In general the comments made by interviewees about the need for bail support schemes were favourable, although criticism highlighted a lack of good feedback. Prosecutors commented that 'rehabilitation has a place in the bail process', and in one area had taken an active interest in supporting the work of a bail support provider by sitting on the management board. Magistrates and clerks were generally very supportive of the idea. One magistrate gave the advice that 'A good bail support scheme must relate to the offence before the court' because 'part of the bail decision is also whether or not a person is likely to be guilty – to weigh up the evidence against them.'

Another magistrate commented: 'Bail support could answer some fears – especially lack of work amongst defendants – they need to be kept busy, train for work', and another believed that 'the sooner you work with people [in the criminal justice process] the better'. A clerk added: 'Bail support is seen as rehabilitative, so this is a worthwhile option.'

Where sentencers were critical it was in not receiving enough feedback about specific clients in particular, and from bail support in general. They remained ignorant of the success or otherwise of bail support work, and this made it harder for them to use this option with confidence.

The feedback from the eleven clients interviewed was very positive. Generally they valued the opportunity to improve their circumstances before sentence, and saw the bail support officers as a genuine source of support and guidance.

Overall, feedback was very positive about the need for bail support, almost universal in acknowledging a place for it in the criminal justice process, and critical more on the lack of explanatory material and generalized feedback than of the need for or known elements of the current scheme.

Lack of feedback and evaluation

There were key weaknesses identified by managers, practitioners and magistrates, most of which were attributed to the lack of common methods of evaluation and accountability. Those points at which a more systematic means of delivery was found to be missing were as follows.

There was generally no particular standard mechanism for ensuring first contact after release from court. There was no standard definition of supervision in terms of its content length and frequency, and no standard means of evaluating adherence to supervision other than attendance. There were also no standard mechanisms for reporting bail support progress to pre-sentence report authors, or any standard mechanism for reporting back to the court on the conduct of defendants on bail support.

Evidence

If these were the weaknesses in the collecting of systematic data, though, the strengths were apparent in the generally very favourable statistical records that were available for some schemes. Although there was a lack of good evaluative material, there were for some projects either a recent inspection report or a statistical analysis of the outcomes that had been recorded. For example, see the data in table 3.3.

Table 3.3 Statistics on bail support (area 3, 1998)

Number of bail supportees for whom bail information was offered to the court: 250

Court decision

Remanded in custody	40%
Bail support	49%
Other	11%

Outcome

Reoffended	4%
Breached	27%
Successful completion	68%

This shows the success rate of a bail support scheme in terms of those returned to court having completed their bail support programme without breach and not having re-offended. This does not take account of the quality of supervision or adherence to anything other than attendance at supervision, but nevertheless the success rate was good if we consider that the target group were those for whom bail was already a risky option. The reconviction rate is low and the absconding, although concerning, is lower than that identified above for general bail by Raine and Willson.

The figures for this scheme are similar to those available for another scheme in a different probation area (given in table 3.4).

Table 3.4 Statistics on bail support (area 2, 1997)

Number referred for bail support	234
Accepted as suitable	59%

Outcome to date

Reoffended	5%
Breached	8%
Breached other bail conditions	17%
Successful completion	68%

In order to examine more closely the mechanisms and detail of these schemes and to look closely at an as yet under-researched part of probation activity, we turn to the issue of partnership.

Pre-trial services 3: Partnerships

Management structure and funding: why partnership?

The history of partnership within probation is illustrated well elsewhere (see Her Majesty's Inspectorate of Probation (1997a). In a nutshell, the three probation services researched had responded firstly to the pressure to spend a proportion of their funds on partnerships during the 1980s and latterly to participate more widely in multi-agency work in the community. This history had informed the style and range of work undertaken in partnership with other agencies and this in turn was a factor in determining the character of the bail support work that had evolved through partnership arrangements. In particular a fear was expressed by ACPOs and sentencers in two of the three areas that other organizations might compete for the Probation Service's core work of court duty and offender supervision. This had resulted in much partnership work being carried out on the margins of its core activity. As one ACPO put it, 'If I have a misgiving about partnership it would be that it might be losing us core work. Value for money asks us to identify and stick to our key tasks.' Or, to put it more positively as one magistrate did: 'Partnership is a very welcome idea. X can do bail support and leave probation officers free to supervise offenders. It allows specialism on both sides.'

All of the six bail support projects visited were funded by probation partnership money alone, except for two which had additional funding through a grant in one case and joint funding with social services in another. The ACPOs saw this as good news for pre-trial services in two ways. Firstly, it had allowed probation services to support work which would otherwise have disappeared during the leaner 'value for money' years. Secondly, it has given the arms-length freedom for partners to experiment with and develop a new service in the way that a new idea needs. As noted in the introduction, 'social work values' or 'advising, assisting and befriending' were seen, for better or worse, to have been preserved in these projects because of the staffing and philosophy of the partner agencies. As some respondents variously commented, 'We were providing through the partnership a number of aspects to a service that would not that been provided otherwise' (ACPO). 'The probation service could not specialize in this area because there are so few cases' (magistrate). 'They (the partner) have the added value of offering services that cater for other parts of the client's life' (bail information officer).

In one way bail support lends itself to this diversity. Like the probation order before the 1991 Criminal Justice Act, bail support is a contract requiring the consent and co-operation of the defendant. Unlike any other area of probation, however, it is dealing with the unconvicted, and therefore requires a philosophy of consent, albeit supported by conditions given some force under the Bail Act. This consent is compatible with the philosophy and methods of voluntary-sector organizations in ways that the court supervision orders are not.

On a more practical level it was also acknowledged that partners could offer closer one-to-one work, in some cases 24-hour cover, and had a close knowledge and working relationship with a number of other organizations with which they also conducted contracted work. For defendants not yet convicted there may also have been a cultural advantage in being supervised by professional staff who were outside the main criminal justice system. Overall, the partnership also added value to the system in providing a commitment and dedication that was testified to in all of the interviews conducted.

With these observations in mind, this sections sets out to examine in more detail the nature of these partnership arrangements, and to examine their effect on bail support work from both sides of the contract.

Who are the partners?

There were two kinds of partner: those involved in co-operation across statutory agencies with a shared aim (police, social services, education and health) and those from the voluntary sector involved in the provision of contracted services. Of the first kind of partnership one area had a fully developed project – for mentally disordered offenders. This was an exemplary scheme, which provided a holistic service to mentally disordered offenders at each point in the criminal justice process, from diversion through bail information and bail support to supervision and throughcare. The scheme involved the co-working of seconded staff from probation, health and social services and had built on the inherent strengths of partnership – varied expertise, easy access to resources from the parent organizations, and speed of decision-making across professional boundaries. This holistic approach to the client group also provided an insight into how the probation service might offer a similar service to all offenders if pre-trial services became part of its core work. There was continuity of access from the client's point of view, and a continuing body of information built up on each client, which was reported to have facilitated quick and effective interventions in court and the good targeting of resources to match need. As one health practitioner put it, 'This is satisfying work and the multi-agency setting is very helpful. We can have a full discussion of each client in confidence and our work here is much more about liaison, assessment and the co-ordination of services.'

Of the four multi-agency partnerships investigated, all involved some measure of liaison and co-operation with police on bail enforcement. For one this was described by an ACPO as a managerial level talk-shop, and in two others there was a chain of communication about specific bailees and routines set up to enforce breach of bail support conditions.

Of the voluntary-sector partners providing bail support in five of the six schemes investigated, all were charitable organizations with existing projects within the probation area. Two were local organizations and the others were branches of national organizations. All had expertise in working with the target client groups of the bail support scheme, but not necessarily any previous experience of bail work or work within the criminal justice sector.

Contracts and funding

The issue of contracts between the probation service as purchaser and the voluntary organizations as providers of bail support programmes was found to be critical in two ways. Firstly it provided a mechanism for quality control (which was not in practice used greatly) and secondly it was an identified source of tension between the agencies.

The contracts between probation as purchaser and the voluntary agencies as providers included common expectations on providing supervision for bailees and to breach for non-compliance, but in other respects there were differences. In one case the money was paid as a block in advance for a set number of bail support packages on an annually renewable contract. In two others the money was paid at set points in the year and was tied to performance and volume of work, and in one other it was purely on a per-client basis.

From the Probation Service's point of view, as expressed by two ACPOs, a tight control of spending prevented any possibility of an overspend and gave flexibility in changing, increasing or decreasing their spending on bail support from year to year. This was seen by the two partner agency managers interviewed as counter-productive in the sense of causing great difficulties for the providers. This was understandably a point of great contention for providers, who expressed particular dismay at the uncertainty of these arrangements. In an interview with the manager of a pre-trial bail support project in area 1, the issue of funding was raised and, in particular, the dominant and controlling position of the Probation Service. The need of the voluntary sector to raise funds to continue to exist, it was felt, put them in a relatively powerless position in negotiating contracts. As the manager put it, 'The statutory agency tends to be the oppressive partner in the partnership. Their practice is oppressive. The voluntary sector is taken for granted.'

They pointed to similar arrangements with other purchasers in social services who offered five-year contracts. This, they maintained, offered the opportunity to make plans for their service, and to invest more constructively in the recruitment and training of staff. The short-termism of the probation contracts might therefore affect the calibre, commitment and quality of staff who could be retained, and prove counter-productive in terms of value for money. This is an area in which more research might be illuminating.

Another area of contention was the number of clients to be supervised within the terms of the contract. In every case the referrals made to the partner exceeded the number anticipated in the contract by as much as 30 per cent over a twelve-month period, meaning that the partners were actually providing more than they were paid for. This was exacerbated in one area by subsequent disputes over mileage claims which officers ran up in order to visit all of these extra clients. It should be remembered that the setting of ceilings on client numbers was not in the hands of the partner, and came down to the number of referrals made by bail information officers on a day-to-day basis. In each area visited there was no mechanism for signalling when the contracted number of referrals had been reached. The bail information officers would continue to refer on the logical grounds of suitability, and the partner would continue to work with those sent. As one bail project supervisor said, 'Arguably we should place a ceiling on sixty (referrals) but this would not be in the spirit of partnership. We would lose goodwill and it would be inefficient, and we would be out of operation for part of the year.'

In another area, despite providing services for more than the contracted number of clients, the partner had to apply for 20 per cent of its funding at the end of the financial year with no automatic guarantee of success. A probation manager who acknowledged that described this sorry picture: 'The contract is a strict one and probation staff are not aware enough of the need to work with their partners to fulfil it. The contract between provider and probation was problematic, and both sides nearly fell out over it.' Or, as one provider manager said, 'We need far more flexibility in funding. There is a very dogmatic approach and a Spanish inquisition if targets are exceeded.' These tensions were universally reported in two areas, and in the third difficulties over funding were reported though within the context of greater respect and co-operation between purchaser and provider.

Communication and organization

Organizational issues differed from partner to partner in ways that there was not time to explore fully, and which are not central to this study. The elements of organization that were significant and which are discussed here were those of staffing and recruitment, breach and enforcement, and communication.

Recruitment and training

It has already been noted above that the funding arrangements put partners under great pressure in recruiting. The lack of money, and uncertainty of income, make recruitment and retention difficult, though the two service managers interviewed both expressed a commitment to finding staff who were committed. Those employed were often qualified already as teachers, social workers or counsellors. The main criteria for selection were commitment and sympathy with the philosophical aims of the organization. The partners in two areas had no staff dedicated to the bail support work but allocated cases to its full- and part-time staff who also worked with other young people through other contract work. One organization tried to recruit part-time sessional staff in order to match the pro-rata nature of the contract, but rejected this in favour of full-time staff. 'We tried sessional workers for weekend visits, but the relationships did not work, so it fell down.' Clients now see the same member of staff throughout, so the quality and effectiveness are better – 'there is just a better motivation and commitment than with sessional workers.'

One of the great benefits of the partnership identified by partner agencies was the availability of training with the probation service, and in all three areas training was available to partner staff as part of their induction and development.

They came from a teaching, social work and counselling back-ground and had received further training from NACRO since starting. They defined their approach as a social work service based on building a relationship with offenders. The service pro-vided supervision to bailees which was based around defined social need and had no set pattern or time, except that some kind of contact, however brief, was expected each week. One strength of the scheme was that bail support supervisors travelled to the clients wherever they lived within each petty sessional division, and an escort to court was provided to ensure return for trial.

In area 3 there was still no clear definition of bail support super-vision, however, and this still relied strongly on the individual work of the bail support staff employed by the voluntary-sector providers. Their definition of bail support supervision varied from client to client, with no consistent application of frequency, length or focus.

Communication

Communication was seen as an essential component of pre-trial work by a number of the bail support officers interviewed, and yet poor communications and lack of good co-operation on the supply and sharing of information were frequently cited as a failing of the projects in all three areas. For example, partner bail support workers reported a lack of communication and interest in bail support work from probation officers. They reported that informa-tion about bailees was frequently not passed across to them when known, and that reports on defendants on bail support were not used by court supervision teams when reporting to the court on defendants. In areas 1 and 2 there were no systems for including feedback on bail support to probation officers preparing pre-sentence reports. A hostel manager also complained that hostel staff prepared detailed reports on bailees supervised by the hostel, which were not systematically referred to in pre-sentence reports.

Although communication and co-operation were expectations across the parts of the service, lack of clarity or line management accountability were reported by two SPOs to be particularly responsible for undermining their effectiveness. There were also mixed reports on the success of computerized information systems which two areas had developed. One area had a dedicated system that facilitated many aspects of the bail information and support processes, and another area used the standardized systems CRAMS. Inevitably the quality and timeliness of the information put in was still inconsistent because of the varying commitment of the probation officers responsible, but this again reflected a management problem rather than a fault of the particular systems.

A specialized computerized probation record system had not been implemented at all in area 1. The partner agency and two bail information officers in particular thought that easier access to client records would improve the effectiveness of their pre-trial work.

There was one aspect of pre-trial work in which communication was reported by two ACPOs to be improving – that between the probation service and the police. There was management-level co-operation in two areas between probation and police on bail and pre-trial issues, and in operation there was a flow of fast and relevant information about offending on bail and breach of bail conditions. In the context of Raine and Willson's (1996) critical study of bail enforcement this was encouraging. They suggested:

> Enforcement practices in the five areas studied were generally acknowledged by the police to be at best patchy. Much criticism was expressed at the unenforceability of certain conditions such as exclusion from city centres. Even apparently enforceable conditions were not backed up with immediate action in the event of non-compliance. There was doubt about information being transmitted from court to the police station nearest the defendant. Any emphasis on co-operation must be welcomed.

In two of the three areas steps had been taken to address this gap. There were mechanisms for communication and co-operation on enforcement between police and probation, particularly in reporting alleged breaches of bail conditions or suspected offending whilst on bail. This was proving helpful according to two of the three ACPOs (the third area had no scheme of this kind). It was also welcomed by two magistrates in particular whose chief fears on bail were, as in previous studies (see Burrows et al. 1994), still largely concerned with enforcement and risk of reoffending or absconding on bail.

Organization

Organization of bail support within the partnerships was similar across the areas. Once a bail support order had been made, bailees were contacted and supervised according to the court's terms until their return to court for sentence. Within these general parameters however, the level of contact, the content and purpose of the supervision of the bailee, and the terms of enforcement were not defined closely or consistently in practice. Similarly the mechanisms for communication about the bailees between supervisor and police, court and probation service were ill defined and, according to many of those interviewed, were not adequate. The effectiveness of these arrangements is therefore discussed next in an evaluation of the schemes.

Outcome and evaluation

Practice in defining and collecting information about the quality and substance of bail support work (as opposed to the number of clients worked with) was diverse. In this respect the downside of a lack of probation control became apparent. If we take for example the central issue of the implementation of bail support supervision plans there were no obvious mechanisms for monitoring consistency or quality. As noted above, each partner recruited its own staff and had, with some additional training from the host probation service, its own internal mechanisms for supervising and training them. In response to questions about the content of bail support supervision, managers, practitioners and clients all reported that the content, timing and frequency of the sessions varied widely from session to session and from officer to officer. The overall approach as described by bail support supervisors was very much the counselling, advocacy role of the old 'advise, assist and befriend' ethos. It had more in common with the professional independence of old-style probation officers, and less with the trained, accountable service focused on national standards which developed during the 1990s. As one supervisor said,

> The onus in probation is on getting the client to comply but we take a paternalistic, helping role. We take a holistic approach and try to make people aware of client needs. We don't see ourselves as providers of all, but we do see ourselves as a link for clients to other services.

None of the service contracts contained any mechanism for prescribing or checking the work of their partner in these respects. The only criteria were numbers supervised and numbers returned to court. It seemed ironic that the universally restrictive nature of the contracts with partners were correspondingly open-ended in terms of quality. One probation manager described them in critical terms: 'Probation staff are not aware of the contract or its implications. There is no guarantee of co-operation or compliance, and the referral mechanism is rather crude and ill defined.'

This is not to say that a commitment to quality was not important for the providers. The commitment and dedication of staff was clear, and the feedback from clients interviewed was very positive about the 'supportive' nature of their experience, the 'opportunity' that it gave at a critical time, and the sympathetic quality of supervision sessions. The overall results in reducing offending on bail and ensuring attendance at court, examined elsewhere in this chapter, are evidence of the success of these projects. It is more a difference in culture between partner and probation service that may, if pre-trial work were to expand, need closer attention. In particular, the issue of enforcement.

Enforcement

This was another aspect of the partnerships that differed from the prevailing climate in probation supervision. When three or more bail supervision sessions were missed, the defendant should be breached, but practice in this area seemed to rely heavily on the discretion of the supervising bail support worker. It was not clear what constituted a failure, what was an acceptable excuse and how swift a move to breach would be. As it was put by one partner manager, 'breaching was not high on the supervisor's list of priorities' for a number of reasons. It was not part of the culture of the voluntary-sector organizations for which they worked, it contradicted their supportive relationship with defendants and it was thought to detract from the successful completions on which their contracts depended. Add to this the lack of clarity or monitoring in the contract, and it was not surprising that the impression within and without was one of 'flexibility' on this issue, much in the style of pre-national standards probation supervision. If this gives sentencers less confidence in bail support, as two magistrates reported from their experience, it is worth noting that in one respect the schemes had a high level of enforcement – namely the business of getting defendants back to court. All the schemes researched put an absolute priority on this and provided an escort to court to ensure compliance. This was always noted as a priority by practitioners and may account for the high level (68–70 per cent) success in completion of bail support programmes. This contrasts with more than 45 per cent of defendants who reportedly broke conditions on bail, and 85 per cent in one study who anticipated that bail conditions would not be enforced (Raine and Willson 1995).

Partnership: five key points

- Partners in crime. Bail support is almost exclusively delivered through partnership, either in collaboration with social services and health or directly through probation partnership money.
- Money worries. A key point of contention for service providers is the restrictive and inflexible funding arrangement that the probation service operates. This makes recruitment and retention of staff difficult and therefore affects the quality of service.
- Training. An advantage for partners is access to training from the probation service for its bail support officers. Training is expensive for them yet is essential for developing a consistent and high-quality service.
- The knowledge. The expertise and flexibility of working practices of partner organizations in working with young offenders is a strong selling point, and justifies their use for probation managers.
- The buck does not stop here. The largest potential problem for these schemes is the inconsistency of breach and enforcement practices.

Pre-trial services 4: bail hostels

It is widely acknowledged (HMIP 1999) that bail hostels are a more widely and firmly established part of the pre-trial world than the other services discussed above. They also have surer funding and national support at policy and practice levels. Nevertheless their role in pre-trial work is under-researched in some regards, particularly in the range of programmes and activities that they run in addition to the standard curfew and accommodation for which they are chiefly used by the courts. There was also some evidence from this study that their contribution to pre-trial work is both underappreciated and underused by others within and without the probation service.

The scope and content of the work of bail hostels has been covered in some detail in the HMI inspection report on hostels (HMIP 1999). There is therefore no need for that to be reproduced here. This section of the chapter will therefore be confined to a brief examination of two closely relevant questions: what contribution do hostels make to the pre-trial process, and what is the scope for using them more? These questions will be answered using the same format as in the sections above, and returned to in the conclusion.

Management structure and funding

Hostels do have advantages over their other pre-trial relations in that their place in the probation world has been secured for longer. This is largely because hostels are funded directly from the Home Office and so do not have to compete for probation formula funding with other elements of probation work. They have also been established nationally since the 1970s and have the advantages of a growing body of expertise, research and support groups within and without the probation service. They also have their own national standards and key performance indicators, which secure their place in probation management planning, and sentencers and others within the court and prison system are aware of their services.

Hostels also have an established place in the bail process on which other aspects of pre-trial services currently rely. Bailees on bail support programmes in all three areas were bailed to hostels as part of the security of their bail package. Hostels were responsible for accommodating a significant proportion of those on bail support programmes. In one area a third of those on bail support were accommodated in hostels. Both central bail officers interviewed described hostels as an essential part of the bail information officers' argument for bail in many marginal cases.

In management terms each service area had a different structure for hostels, though with one common thread. Despite their place in the court process, they were managed through the ACPO for prisons or special services, and not with pre-trial work or court services. This may have accounted for some of the difficulties which the hostel managers identified in communicating effectively with community supervision and court teams (see below).

Communication and organization

A number of points emerged from this research about hostels that are of relevance to the study of pre-trial services. Firstly, a number of programmes had been established in hostels which were designed, like bail support, to tackle offending through assisting or confronting the problems of defendants. Each of the five hostels visited across the three probation areas offered drug counselling, employment education and training programmes, group therapy, individual support work and structured leisure activities. Each had a regular timetable of visits with an event or surgery or counselling session each day, supplemented by a regular programme of groupwork to discuss current issues including living skills and tackling offending. Feedback on these regimes from nine hostel residents interviewed at two hostels was very positive (see evaluation below).

Secondly, these programmes were supported effectively by the contracted services of professionals and volunteers who provided expertise on employment, leisure and addiction. The regime at two hostels in particular was a model of inter-agency partnership and offered a range of services for residents that were delivered by visiting professionals from the health and voluntary sectors. The hostels were proactive about identifying and meeting the criminogenic needs of their residents. One hostel manager described the need in particular to tackle the problems of drug addiction which were the most likely indicator of reconviction and failure to rehabilitate:

Defendants will hide their addiction to get bail. We need to set up guidelines for managing drug users in hostels. I would like to see drug users assessed by experts and clear conditions attached to bail for opiate users. It would be effective if we could have a compulsory week in custody on de-tox before hostel admission.

On mentally disordered offenders one manager was equally clear on the potential of hostels to meet need if the service could be provided: 'A specialized hostel service could be more effective. Mentally disordered offenders in particular need a dedicated hostel. Their problems are camouflaged in mixed hostels and they need medication expertise.'

Thirdly, like bail support, the range of work undertaken at hostels was not fully recognized by the magistrates interviewed, three of whom assumed that hostels were uniform in their supervision and provided a curfew and accommodation only. Two sentencers were more aware of hostel regimes and commented, 'Hostel decisions carry weight because we are aware of the thorough assessment before accepting.' However, it was also a common theme amongst clerks, prosecutors and magistrates that although hostels were known of, the precise detail of their regimes was not known. As one magistrate said, 'There is a place for bail support – rehabilitation would be useful in the bail process. But there is a lack of information about hostels. We need to know what is going on in hostels and what is on offer.'

Fourthly, hostel staff and managers also reported poor communication with the rest of the probation service. In spite of the range of work undertaken and expertise which hostels have developed, hostel managers reported a sense of being marginalized by the probation service generally. They reported a lack of respect for hostel work and cited the difficulty in getting hostel reports included in pre-sentence reports by court team probation officers. 'We are perceived as having unqualified staff and poor practice. Hostels are not seen as part of the overall probation structure.' The lack of knowledge about hostel work was also seen as counterproductive to the referral process. One manager said that poor referrals were undermining the success of the hostels. 'Forty per cent of those bailed to the hostel do not arrive. Targeting is haphazard and needs more thought. The hostel is wrongly seen as a last-chance saloon – for up-tariff and severe cases only.'

Communication

Poor communication was an issue raised by hostel staff in two ways. Poor referral information about potential and new residents was believed to be undermining the assessment process and causing management problems in coping with unsuitable residents. Secondly, hostels perceived in probation officers a lack of interest in information about residents from hostels, which was leading to valuable knowledge about defendants being missed from pre-sentence reports.

On the first point the four hostel managers interviewed had clear and strong views on the assessment process by which bailees were selected. In two of the three probation areas referrals to hostels were controlled by central bail referral officers, but in all cases the original referral and assessment of defendants was made by bail information officers at court. Hostel managers were critical of what they saw as the shortfalls in this service, leading to missed or inappropriate referrals: 'Assessment at court is not up to it – we are not getting the right people. All those denied bail by police and the CPS should be interviewed. Assessment by bail information officers is not enough.' On the point of safety and risk management: 'The bail information officer sometimes says no to drugs being a problem, but the resident turns out on arrival to be an

---

Hostels: five key points

- Under a bushel. Magistrates were generally unaware that hostels currently offer a high level of programmes for bailees including offence-focused group work, drug counselling and training.
- Missed target. Low success rates in bail hostels are largely due to non-arrival from court. Forty per cent of those bailed do not arrive. Those that do, tend to succeed.
- Partners in crime. Hostels work closely with defendants on bail support. Many are accommodated in hostels whilst receiving other help from visiting bail support officers.
- Customer support. Bailees in hostels were pleasantly surprised at the supportive atmosphere and very positive about the opportunity to 'put their lives together' in their weeks before sentence.
- Communication breakdown. Hostel managers reported feeling unfairly relegated to the margins of probation work. Hostel insights and positive work with bailees seldom appeared in pre-sentence reports.

addict.' 'Risk criteria for bail are not properly applied. There is too short a time (at court) to take decisions which fully recognize the risk to other residents and to the public in the area, or to consider the risk of harm.'

The call was not for less bail information but for more emphasis on it. Hostel managers were asking for their role to be more professional with a thorough assessment process with more time and resources with which to do it.

Evaluation and assessment

A thorough assessment of hostel performance is available in the HMIP inspection report, and targeting has produced a range of tools and information by which success rates at hostels can and have been evaluated. This more limited study can therefore add little to that debate. Hostels' potential role in bail support is more relevant here and not reported elsewhere. In two of the three probation areas accommodation was provided for a third of defendants on bail support, and they offered a range of programmes for bailees which made up part of the bail support programme. As one hostel manager suggested, the model of bail support packages offered by hostels in most probation areas could provide a worthwhile starting-point for services without bail support schemes to begin to develop them, using existing resources and expertise from their own hostels. The gap in credibility with courts was more one of lack of information than of poor performance. All of the sentencers interviewed welcomed the services that hostels offered and said that they would support them and use them if they had more information about them.

In discussing the success of hostels with bailees, hostel managers and staff were critical of the bail information and bail process generally. As reported above, they reported that 40 per cent of those bailed failed to appear at the hostel, and that of those who arrived, too high a proportion had undetected addiction problems. This was said by one manager to be an explanation for poor success rates with bailees in some hostels; with those who did arrive, success was high, 85 per cent completing their bail period without absconding or being charged with further offences. This compares favourably with the Raine and Willson (1995) figures quoted earlier.

Feedback from hostel residents

As noted above, feedback from hostel residents was positive. In discussion with two groups of residents, the themes that emerged were that the hostel was both more demanding and more helpful than they had anticipated. A regime of participation in pro-grammes and group meetings was discussed, and as one resident commented, 'Staff treat you with respect. There is a strict regime. Rules are needed. If you miss a meeting you can't go on Friday [on the leisure outings].' One said that he 'feared the hostel experience but actually I found the experience positive. Sentencers don't see this as a punishment but it is.' Another commented: 'It gives you the opportunity to consider life and make plans – better than a remand in custody. For reoffending on bail there is a big threat.'

Overall, the possibility of using hostels as a core element of any pre-trial service seemed very clear. The structure (supervised accommodation, specialist staff, links across the criminal justice network) and the availability (hostels in each probation area and linked to every court) offer a basis on which to build a bail support programme in any probation area that lacks one. The resources are there for bail support packages that include supervision, accom-modation and support that will answer both the needs of defend-ants and the expressed wishes of sentencers.

Conclusion

The difficulties in presenting the material collected for this chapter reflect the climate in which the projects were formed. As chapter 2 has argued, the history of the development of pre-trial work in this country has been left to a few pioneers with small budgets in a largely unsupportive environment. Their work is therefore often local in character and difficult to quantify because of a lack of consistent methods and standards. In the absence of central support or core funding, pre-trial services are a result, as Sue Winfield puts it in chapter 5, of the work of a number of dedicated and enthusiastic managers and practitioners who were 'flying the flag' during the difficult years in which hypothecated funding was withheld. They therefore deserve some credit for existing at all.

What was found, consequently, were pockets of imaginative and innovative practice which had some distinct characteristics. Firstly there were examples of bottom-up work which had developed in many cases from the work of enthusiastic practitioners or managers within the probation service. Secondly, because most bail support work was found to involve partnership, there were voluntary-sector-operated services. These were characterized by multi-agency work and filled some of the gaps in what is now being called 'joined-up policy', between criminal justice and social work agencies. Thirdly, because of the necessary consent of unconvicted 'clients' and the involvement of voluntary-sector partners, the pre-trial work investigated was frequently characterized as 'client-centred' in its approach to offenders and their social problems. It was found in some respects to reflect, for better or worse, the values and methods of the 'old' pre-national standards probation service. Lastly, in a climate of inter-agency partnership, best value and a national drive for bail information schemes in all courts, there were examples of top-down management-led work characterized by an emphasis on targets, value for money and crime reduction.

This chapter has attempted to present a picture of the range and diversity of the work found as well as the themes that emerged. The work must stand by itself as a model which other services may wish to copy or adapt. What might be more useful here is simply to reflect on the themes which emerged and to consider them briefly in the context of what we have called a 'remand management strategy'.

Firstly the positives. The strengths lie in the commitment of the staff, the usefulness of the underlying idea and the partnerships that have developed to nurture it. It is worth repeating that, across the projects, there was almost universal support for the notion of pre-trial work amongst all ranks and professions interviewed who had some direct involvement or contact with the work. There was also very good evidence of success where records or evaluations had been made. The work also seemed to fit in well with other elements of the criminal justice process without duplication or conflict. In short, it was effective and welcome, and added value to the bail process, whether assessed according to a humanitarian, cost-effective or risk-management viewpoint.

The negatives or weaknesses of the process were more operational and reflected more on the prevailing climate and weaknesses in the criminal justice system than on the notion of pre-trial work itself. A negative theme was the lack of good communication between the relevant parts of the criminal justice system, both within the Probation Service and particularly across the agencies – notably between bail information teams in court and prison, and between bail support staff and community supervision teams. Hostel managers also reported this perception of marginalization and isolation. General access to computerized probation records was seen as an answer, but in all three areas doubt was expressed at how effectively utilized computerization had been. Essentially, it was reported that records were not being completed systematically or in time by probation officers to be of value to other users.

A lack of clear targets and good evaluative data was a hindrance to the research, as said above, but also as a means of tracking and improving the work itself. Although basic data on numbers of clients served was commonly kept, little in the way of information existed to be able to evaluate the effectiveness of the pre-trial services examined, either in the contracts with partner agencies, routine data collection or internal/external evaluation. Both bail support and bail information schemes had some records of success in the limited task of persuading sentencers to follow a particular recommendation, but there was very little information with which to assess the success of that choice. Records of successful returns to court for trial were kept and the results were favourable, but there is a need for more measurement of whether pre-trial work can reduce offending in both the long and the short term. Moreover, to support and expand pre-trial work it is hoped that managers will see the need for a more consistent set of guidelines and standards for this work to ensure the most efficient and effective use of resources. It is hoped that policy-makers will support that process by including targets and performance indicators for pre-trial work, which secure for it both funding and respect within the Probation Service.

Lastly, and most importantly, it is hoped that those within and without the criminal justice system will see a need for what has been argued elsewhere in this book as a 'comprehensive remand management strategy'. The research findings point strongly to the need for such a co-ordinated approach, with set expectations of the Probation Service's role within the context of the work of the court, police and prison services. The Probation Service has the skills and resources to build an effective bail support and bail information service with strategies for accommodation and inter-agency partnership. This will rely in turn on the work of the courts, the Crown Prosecution Service, the police and the prisons in order to work safely and effectively in the interests of the public. Each service has a crucial role to play in the management of defendants pre-trial, and this is best served by clarity of purpose and role, co-operation, good communication and secure access to reliable information.

4. The Potential Scope for Remand Services

The previous chapter demonstrated the range of successful work which continues to be carried on by the Probation Service in England and Wales. It also placed on record the enduring commitment of staff to this work, as well as suggesting ways in which existing gains could be strengthened still further and difficulties addressed. This chapter aims to build on this exploration of the local and the specific by addressing the issue of more general applicability. It asks the question: what is the potential contribution that an active remand management strategy can make to a reduction in the numbers of adults remanded to custody? To address this question, a small study was undertaken in a large magistrates' court. A random sample of court records was examined and information concerning court decision-making and relevant offender and offence data was extracted. The aim of this study was to explore the factors associated with denial of bail (evaluating the significance of, for example, the seriousness of the offence) and the reasons magistrates openly state for denial of bail in order to determine the scope for probation interventions in changing these decisions through the provision of information or a range of remand services.

As this chapter will demonstrate, in this study every effort was made to collect comprehensive data on the pre-trial process based on a very thorough examination of the information collected in existing court records. We shall show, however, that there are deficiencies in these data which reflect the relative neglect of this important area of court decision-making; a finding which, in itself, has helped to form the conclusions of this study.

The bail provisions

When a defendant appears in court, it is possible for the case to be dealt with through to the conclusion of sentencing in one sitting. In such circumstances no further so-called 'pre-trial' decisions are necessary. It is far more common, however, for the court not to be able to proceed to sentence on this first occasion, and for the case to be adjourned to a future date. In these circumstances, magistrates must decide whether to remand the defendant on bail or in custody until the case returns before the court (usually for periods of one week at a time). Where a case is adjourned, magistrates have three basic options:

- To remand the defendant in custody until the next court hearing.
- To grant the defendant conditional bail, that is, bail in the community but with certain specific restrictions on the defendant's behaviour or liberty.
- To grant the defendant unconditional bail, with the requirement that he or she must appear at the specified future court hearing.

The grounds on which the court can refuse bail are set out in the Bail Act 1976, the main ones being the court believes that:

- The defendant will fail to appear at the next court hearing or 'surrender to custody'.
- The defendant is likely to commit further offences while on bail.
- The defendant is likely to interfere with the witnesses who will be giving evidence against them, or obstruct the course of justice.

The Bail Amendment Act 1993 gave the Crown Prosecution Service the right to appeal a magistrates' decision to grant bail, provided objections to bail were made at the original hearing. Hucklesby (1997a), however, found that these powers were rarely used, as magistrates rarely went against CPS objection to bail (see also Raine and Willson 1996).

The grounds for refusing bail were further extended by the Criminal Justice and Public Order Act 1994, which introduced six new measures restricting the use of bail and increasing the courts' powers to deal with breach of bail conditions or offending on bail. Three of these new measures related to police powers, and three concerned the courts:

- A defendant charged with murder, attempted murder, rape, attempted rape or manslaughter who has a previous conviction for any of these offences, may not be granted bail but must be remanded in custody (section 25).

- No presumption is to be made in favour of bail for a defendant charged with an indictable or either-way triable offence if it appears that the defendant was on bail at the time these offences were committed (section 26).
- Courts may, on application from the prosecution, reconsider a bail decision before a defendant's next scheduled court hearing where new evidence relevant to the bail decision has come to light, and impose or vary bail conditions, or revoke bail (section 30).

The Crime and Disorder Act 1998 introduced four new measures concerning bail:

- Courts may require any person granted bail to give a security (section 54.1).
- Courts were given increased powers to demand forfeiture of a security (section 55).
- Courts may impose a condition of bail that requires the defendant to attend an interview with a legal adviser (section 54.2).
- Section 56 of the 1998 Act provides for a rebuttal of the presumption against bail introduced in section 25 of the Criminal Justice and Public Order Act 1994 (see above).

It is important to remember, however, notwithstanding the amendments to the Bail Act 1976, that bail is not technically granted, it is denied. A defendant has a right not to be held in custody, but to be granted bail. Thus bail can only be refused if the court is satisfied that an exception to the general right to bail exists (Gibson 1995). In making its bail decision the court must balance the presumption in favour of bail (where it exists, see below) with the following considerations (see McLean et al. 1995: 43):

- the nature and seriousness of the offence
- the character and antecedents, associations and community ties of the defendant
- the defendant's previous behaviour on bail
- the strength of the evidence.

There is no general presumption in favour of bail where a defendant has been convicted of an offence, although bail may be granted in this circumstance. In practice a bail decision only needs to be made if the court is unable to proceed directly to sentencing after a determination of guilt. This situation is most likely to arise where the court is considering a community or custodial sentence and where reports are required. Under these circumstances, even where a court has to be satisfied that a custodial sentence is the only proper disposal, the court must have very good reasons for refusing bail prior to submission of reports (McLean et al. 1995: 41–2).

In all cases there is a presumption in favour of unconditional bail. No conditions may be attached to bail unless they are necessary to prevent occurrences of those events or actions for which bail may be denied (see above). If these circumstances are met, the court may impose conditions to bail, including: to report to a designated police station at specified times, to comply with a curfew, to reside at a given address (including an approved hostel), not to associate with a victim, and to stay away from a specified location. If a court withholds bail or imposes conditions to bail, it must give its reasons for doing so and record a note of its decision (McLean et al. 1995: 46).

Methodology

In ideal terms, a study of remand or bail decision-making should be undertaken in real time, that is, a researcher should be present in court to ensure that all relevant information is systematically and independently recorded. This approach was, however, beyond the resources available to this research and a retrospective study of court records was identified as the only viable method. A large metropolitan court was selected for this study to provide a sufficiently large population from which to draw a representative sample of decision-making, reflecting the full range of offences, defendants and outcomes. The sample was limited to adult offenders, as bail provisions and services concerning juveniles are different, and to those dealt with exclusively in the magistrates' court (that is, Crown Court cases were excluded).

The court in which this study was based maintained both a computerized and a paper-based system of record keeping. In the main, sentencing data were computerized, while information about court processing was contained in paper-based case files. Once final sentencing had taken place the complete set of paper files relating to each case were lodged in box files – each containing about sixteen cases. An average of seventy-two boxes were filled per month, 864 per year, covering all cases dealt with in the court.

The research was based on the most up-to-date sample for which full information was available. A period of twelve months was selected from March 1998 to February 1999 (from when the data collection took place). A random sample of one in nine boxes was drawn, yielding on average eight boxes per month. Each box file contained, on average, sixteen sets of green folders containing the case papers relating to the processing of an individual case. The case files in each box were examined and matters relating to motoring offences, council tax default and those remitted to the Crown Court were excluded. Cases containing obvious instances of incomplete information or missing papers were also excluded. Only cases involving indictable offences were selected for this study. In total, ninety-six boxes contained relevant and usable case papers, from which a usable sample of 130 cases was derived.

Cases which were eligible for this study were those relating to indictable offences, dealt with exclusively in the magistrates' court and where a complete set of papers was contained in the file (providing the necessary information). All cases which met these criteria were included in the study.

A pro forma was drawn up to record relevant information about each case (Figure 4.1). The pro forma was developed following a small pilot study of court records to determine what information courts routinely collected concerning the processing and sentencing of individual cases. All relevant and available information contained in the court records was taken directly from the case file and recorded directly on the pro forma (see below) for each individual case. Sentencing information was tracked through the courts' computerized record system and the main sentencing outcome was added to the pro forma. Approximately 5 per cent of cases were eliminated from the sample at this stage as no sentencing data could be traced. Where relevant, the number of weeks a defendant spent on remand in custody was calculated and recorded on the pro forma.

The court did not routinely record information in case files concerning the defendants' sex or ethnic origin, and as it was not possible to discern this information accurately from other sources, no such recording has been possible.

```
Bail and Remand Case Recording Pro forma

Court date: ..........................        Ref No: ......................................

Name: ...............................         Age/DoB: .................................

Main Offence: ......................          Previous convictions: ..................
Other offences:                              ...............................................
....................................................................................................
....................................................................................................

Police bail decision: RIC □    Conditional bail □    U/C bail □

Court bail decision:   I RIC □    Conditional bail □    U/C bail □
                       2 RIC □    Conditional bail □    U/C bail □
                       3 RIC □    Conditional bail □    U/C bail □

Court reasons for bail or remand decision:
Commit further offences              □
Interfere with witnesses             □
Seriousness of offence               □
Fail to appear                       □
Previous conduct on bail             □
Other ...............................................................................

Bail conditions imposed and reasons:
UCB              □          Reside at                    □
Report police    □          Not to contact               □
Hostel           □          Other .........................................
Curfew           □          RIC                          □

Number of weeks held on Remand in Custody: .............

Final main sentencing outcome: ...................................................
```

Figure 4.1

Data collection was completed between February and June 1999. The information contained in the completed pro formas was coded and transferred into a standard statistical data processing package (SPSS), which was used to analyse and produce the findings from this study. Statistical processing of the data has been limited. Basic tests of significance (to explore whether there is a relationship between two variables, for example, seriousness of offence and bail conditions) could not be conducted on these data. T-tests may only be utilized where the data are interval in nature (that is, the data run in series), whereas information about court decision-making is nominal data (that is, the variables are discrete). Chi-square tests were performed on the data, but found to be invalid as the cell size was less than five in too many instances, and zero in others. It is possible that this problem could have been partly avoided if the sample size was increased by a factor of five, but this would not have corrected the character of the data to produce zero values for certain variables, and thus it is likely that chi-square tests could not be used even for a larger sample size. Multivariate analysis was considered, but like T-tests, this analysis requires interval data and thus could not be used in this study. Under these circumstances the analysis has been undertaken on the basis of cross-tabulations and frequencies.

Basic characteristics of the sample

The sample consisted of 130 adult defendants processed and sentenced in a large metropolitan court between March 1998 and February 1999.

Age

Less than one-fifth of the sample (17.8 per cent) were aged thirty-six and above at the time of sentence. The most common age of

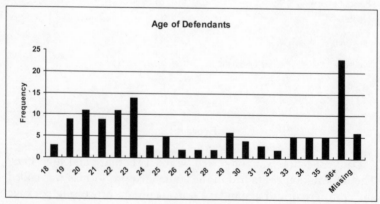

Figure 4.2

defendants was in the range between nineteen and twenty-three years inclusive. This group represented 41.6 per cent of the sample (N = 54).

These findings are consistent with the age profile of defendants appearing in magistrates' courts generally (Flood-Page and Mackie 1998: 132).

Ethnic origin and gender
The case records on which this study was based did not contain any recording of the ethnic origin or gender of defendants, nor could this information be discerned from any other source of information held by the court. A study of sentencing in 3,000 magistrates' courts found that approximately 85 per cent of defendants were male and 15 per cent were female (Flood-Page and Mackie 1998: 132). Although this figure cannot be corroborated from this research it is likely that broadly the same proportions existed in the current sample.

Table 4.1 Ethnic group of cases in magistrates' courts' sample

White	77.8%
Black	11.1%
Asian	7.0%
Other	1.9%
Not known	2.1%

In their study, Flood-Page and Mackie (1998) found the breakdown of ethnic groupings shown in table 4.1. The present study was conducted in a magistrates' court located in a large metropolitan area with relatively high Black and Asian populations. It is likely, therefore, that the number of Black and Asian defendants in this study was higher than the figures reported above.

Offending and offences
The current offences with which defendants were charged, and their previous convictions, were routinely recorded on the court case files. In this study, however, the amount of information recorded was found to vary. For example, in respect of the current charges/offences it was common to find incomplete information concerning the facts of the offence (which may have indicated the severity of the offence) and any other concurrent matters. It was

not possible in this study, therefore, to undertake any analysis of the severity of the offence or to compare, for example, the differences in circumstances between burglary offences or violent offences (which are known to vary widely in severity). For present purposes the main charge/offence was the only consistent data available – and this is shown in table 4.2.

Table 4.2 Main charge/offence

	No.	%
Robbery	1	0.8
GBH	3	2.3
Affray	5	3.8
ABH	43	33.1
Possession of an offensive weapon	2	1.5
Threatening behaviour	6	4.6
Indecent assault	1	.8
Harassment	11	8.5
Drug offences	2	1.5
Criminal damage	7	5.4
Burglary	22	16.9
Theft	24	18.5
Handling stolen goods	1	0.8
Going equipped	1	0.8
Deception	1	0.8

Comparison of the pattern of offences prosecuted in one magistrates' court with national figures can be misleading as average national data do not reflect the range of local circumstances. A comparison of the figures found in this study with a sample drawn from twenty-five magistrates' courts (Flood-Page and Mackie 1998) shows some broad similarities between the offence patterns found in this study and some specific differences. Notably, the rate of violent offences found in this study (at just over 16 per cent) is higher than the average found elsewhere (at about 5 per cent). Although we cannot explain the underlying causes of this difference, it is found in the relatively high proportion of ABH charges – 33.1 per cent of the total. Similarly, we found a higher rate of offences of burglary (about 17 per cent) compared with about 3 per cent found elsewhere. Conversely the rate of prosecution for offences of fraud and drugs was slightly lower in this study than in those courts studied by Flood-Page and Mackie (1998), whereas the rates for theft and criminal damage were broadly similar.

The randomized sampling method, utilized in this study was intended to produce a representative sample of the throughput of defendants and offences in this local court. It is possible that distortions in the information we derived occurred as a result of the sample size (although statistically these should be small), or because of inconsistencies or errors in court record keeping, or because incomplete information was available. Ultimately, however, differences in offence patterns between the court involved in this study and others do not affect the overall findings of this study. This is partly because the average magistrates' court is a statistical phenomenon, but more importantly because, as we go on to show, offence patterns do not appear to be strongly related to bail decision-making.

Previous convictions

Although magistrates are not normally made aware of defendants' previous convictions until sentencing occurs, the court may be made aware of any previous convictions if the prosecution believe these facts have a bearing on the bail decision. It is also inevitable that some defendants are well known to the court, and this knowledge may affect the courts' decision-making. A defendant's previous convictions will be known to probation services and are an important factor to be taken into account in any assessment of the risk to the public the defendant may pose, and the risk of reoffending. A defendant may also have previous experience of supervision and the probation service should take account of behaviour on supervision in planning and putting forward proposals for bail support. In particular the probation service should seek to evaluate the likelihood of successful completion of a period of supervised or unsupervised bail in the community.

Given this relevance of defendants' previous convictions to aspects of bail, this study sought to obtain this information from court case files. These case files routinely contain information about defendants' previous convictions, but the relevant papers were missing or no record of previous convictions were made in over 50 per cent of cases. This extent of missing data meant that it was not possible to include previous convictions in any further analysis.

Other characteristics

A range of additional information may be available to the court in reaching decisions concerning bail. If a defendant is represented by a solicitor or if the probation service provides bail information, then the magistrates are likely to have more information (which may have been verified) than if a defendant is unrepresented. This additional information may include: verification of a permanent address or availability of alternative accommodation, the defendant's employment status and record, the defendant's mental state, her/his family situation and responsibilities, whether the defendant has a record of substance abuse (drugs or alcohol) and criminal or community ties. The defendant's situation in respect of all of these factors has been shown to influence magistrates' decision-making (Morgan and Henderson 1998: 27). For example, stable accommodation and a good employment record may positively influence magistrates towards community bail, whereas a record of substance abuse and criminal ties may influence magistrates towards a remand in custody.

It is not common practice, however, for courts to record any such information in case files. Homelessness or lack of suitable accommodation, for example, has been shown to increase the risk of a custodial remand (Morgan and Henderson 1998: 30), but courts do not make any routine record of the housing status of defendants. Although such factors are clearly important, not only for the bail decision but also for any remand management strategy, it has not been possible directly to include them in this study. Information concerning these factors is only, at best, heard in open court and magistrates' bail decisions are based on their assessment of a wide range of risk and protective factors within the framework of the Bail Act 1976 (as amended) (Morgan and Henderson 1998), as well as being influenced by local custom and practice (Hucklesby 1997b). Magistrates, therefore, make their assessment of the impact of these factors on the defendant's likelihood of further offending, or risk of non-appearance and so on, and these reasons are given for the bail decision. Thus homeless defendants may be refused bail because of the lack of a suitable bail address, but courts tend perhaps routinely to record this as a likelihood of failure to appear.

In the absence of complete and accurate recording of defendants' circumstances and the links between them and the bail decision in the case files, this study was limited to an evaluation of known factors and their influence on magistrates' bail decisions.

Bail or remand outcomes

In the routine operation of magistrates' courts it is the norm for defendants to make a number of appearances before they are finally sentenced. On the basis of the information contained in court case files an estimate of the number of court appearances prior to sentence (that is, the number of occasions on which bail decisions must be made) was produced as in table 4.3.

Table 4.3 Number of court appearances before sentence

	No.	%
1	39	30
2	30	23
3 or more	41	32
Missing	20	15

From the case files, however, it was not possible accurately to track any changes to a defendant's bail status, as the reasons magistrates gave for their bail decision are not specific to any type of decision. In other words, a defendant may be remanded in custody because the magistrates believe the offence is serious enough to merit it, but a defendant may be granted conditional bail on the same grounds. However, from the information contained in the case files it appears that once magistrates have made their first bail decision (whether to remand in custody or grant conditional or unconditional bail) it is rarely changed on subsequent appearances. We cannot estimate, based on court records, the number of instances where bail conditions were subsequently imposed or tightened, or where a subsequent remand in custody occurred; but on only two occasions was a defendant released from a remand in custody to bail in the community. For the purposes of the present study, therefore, information concerning only the magistrates' first bail decision has been used. This data is presented in table 4.4.

Table 4.4 Magistrates' bail decisions

	No.	%
Remand in custody	19	14.6
Conditional bail	25	19.2
Conditional bail (routine conditions)	77	59.2
Unconditional bail	9	6.9

As previously indicated, magistrates have three basic options at the adjournment stage: to grant unconditional bail, to grant bail with conditions or to remand the defendant in custody. When the data from this study were examined, it became apparent that magistrates granted unconditional bail in very few cases (6.9 per cent), but that they appeared almost routinely to attach common bail, conditions (that is, (i) not to contact witnesses, and (ii) to reside at a specified address) to the majority of cases (59.2 per cent). The use of conditional bail in this manner stretches the powers of the courts under the Bail Act 1976 and raises questions as to whether the courts were applying the law in the manner in which it was intended. The routine application of bail conditions is certainly not in keeping with the principles of the Bail Act (that conditions should only be applied to bail where specific reasons are found), but it was very common practice.

For present purposes, therefore, we have separated out those cases where routine conditions appear to have been applied, from other cases of conditional bail where the imposition of conditions appears to reflect more directly the characteristics of the defendant or the charges faced. In the table 4.4, therefore, we have separated out four types of bail decision: (i) remand in custody, (ii) conditional bail, (iii) conditional bail with routine conditions, and (iv) unconditional bail.

Cases dealt with per year

An estimate based on this sample of court records indicates that the court involved in this study dealt with approximately 14,000 indictable cases per year. If the percentages of decision-making found for the research sample are scaled up for the whole court population we obtain the figures given in table 4.5.

Table 4.5 Estimate of magistrates' bail decisions for one year

	%	Estimated number per year
Remand in custody	14.6	2044
Conditional bail	19.2	2688
Conditional bail (routine conditions)	59.2	8288
Unconditional bail	6.9	966

Thus we can see that the total number of adult defendants remanded in custody in one year in a busy metropolitan court is over 2,000. If the court sat on every weekday for the whole year this would mean that, on average, seven adults were remanded in custody daily. The average length of a custodial remand was five weeks.

Reasons for bail decisions
Magistrates must give reasons for their bail decisions and these reasons should be recorded by the court. The criteria magistrates may take into account in reaching their decision, and the reasons they state for refusal of bail or the attachment of conditions to bail are limited to those discussed above. The reasons magistrates in this study gave for their bail decisions are summarized in table 4.6.

Table 4.6 Main reasons for magistrates' bail decisions

	No.	%
Seriousness of the offence	61	46.9
Failure to appear	13	10.0
Likely to commit further offences	13	10.0
Concern for witnesses	9	6.9
Previous conduct on bail	7	5.4
Multiple reasons	7	5.4
Defendant's previous conduct	1	0.8
No reason given	19	14.6

Clearly magistrates relied most heavily on their assessment of the seriousness of the offence in justifying their bail decisions. There are probably few who would argue that offence seriousness is not a relevant factor in the bail decision: offence seriousness is a retrospective factor to the extent that the facts (which may be contested) are known to the court, and it is axiomatic in criminal justice decision-making that seriousness is a major factor. It is not clear, however, from the Bail Act or other research, how far offence seriousness should prevail in bail decisions, or to what extent this factor should be balanced with others. Certainly, however, it seems clear that offence seriousness *of and by itself* does not represent grounds for the refusal of bail. Otherwise, the provisions of the Bail Act add little to an understanding of this process and it may be that appeals taken under the Human Rights Act will prove a more reliable vehicle for providing such clarification.

Although the provisions of the Bail Act 1976 (as amended) were intended to establish criteria for the imposition of conditions to bail, and stiffer criteria for the denial of bail (similar, but less structured, than the 'serious enough' and 'so serious' criteria that must be satisfied before courts may impose a community or custodial sentence), the court in this study did not appear to follow this convention, but instead appeared to select reasons on a more *ad hoc* basis. For example, the court may have denied bail and stated that this decision was based on the seriousness of the offence, but it also granted conditional bail, in some cases, and stated that this decision too was based on the seriousness of the offence. The range of bail decisions and the reasons magistrates gave for their decisions are presented in table 4.7.

The distribution of reasons for magistrates' bail decisions in table 4.7 shows no particular pattern and indicates that the courts' use of reasons is not decision-specific. Thus, any of the reasons for denial of bail or attachment of conditions have been used for the full range of outcomes (see also Hucklesby 1997b). This may, of course, be an indication of appropriate decision-making if, and only if, there is robust and reliable information available to the court in making these decisions and if the outcome (in particular the conditions attached to bail) address the specific concerns of the court and the behaviour of the defendant.

On the basis of the information available in court records it was not possible to test whether there were any links between offence and

Table 4.7 Reasons for bail decision by magistrates' bail decision

	Remand in custody	Conditional bail (with specific conditions)	Conditional bail (with routine conditions)
Seriousness of offence	8 (7.5%)	6 (5.6%)	32 (29.9%)
Fail to appear	0	5 (4.7%)	5 (4.7%)
Commit further offences	5 (4.7%)	2 (1.9%)	13 (12.1%)
Concern for witnesses	3 (2.8%)	0	10 (9.3%)
Previous conduct on bail	2 (1.9%)	6 (5.6%)	1 (0.9%)
No reasons given	1 (0.8%)	6 (5.6%)	16 (12.3%)

offender characteristics and bail decisions. The particular finding that the court appeared almost routinely to apply bail conditions to the majority of defendants, however, suggests that these links are at best tenuous. A further problem arises because some of the reasons for denial of unconditional bail are based, in large part, on guesswork about the likely future behaviour of the defendant (for example, failure to appear at subsequent court hearings, likely to commit further offences), and there is no information about the basis on which magistrates make these assumptions.

In an attempt to explore further this area of court decision-making, an examination of the factors associated with magistrates' bail decisions was undertaken.

Factors associated with magistrates' bail decisions

In any determination of the scope for reducing the number of defendants remanded in custody it is necessary to understand what factors influence magistrates in a refusal of bail. Because of the limitations on the amount and type of information held in court records it has not been possible to identify the offender character-istics that influence this decision. In this study we have been limited to exploring the links between police bail decisions, the seriousness of the offence and final sentencing outcome and bail decisions.

Police bail decisions

Any attempt to explore the links between police bail decisions and subsequent decisions by magistrates is based on the assumption that the criminal justice context and factors associated with these decisions is the same in both cases. In fact this is not straightforwardly the case, and the police bail decision is made in very different circumstances from that of the court. For example, a higher rate of custodial remands is to be expected from the police as defendants are held in custody overnight to be produced at the next available court sitting. Indeed, this expectation is borne out by the findings which show that magistrates granted bail to the majority of those denied bail by the police.

Table 4.8 Police bail decision by magistrates' bail decision

	Remand in custody	Conditional bail (with specific conditions)	Conditional bail (with routine conditions)	Unconditional bail
Remand in custody	14 (11.5%)	8 (6.6%)	12 (9.8%)	0
Conditional bail	1 (0.8%)	5 (4.1%)	42 (34.4%)	3 (2.5%)
Unconditional bail	4 (3.3%)	11 (9.0%)	17 (13.9%)	5 (4.1%)

One might expect a greater degree of congruence, however, between police and magistrates' decisions to apply conditions to bail. A basic examination of the data shows there to be a similarity in the police decision to apply conditions to bail and the subsequent court decision, but the court rarely (in about 13 per cent of cases) gave unconditional bail where the police had done so. In the majority of cases where the police granted unconditional bail the court imposed bail conditions, and in four cases remanded defendants in custody.

On the basis of these results, therefore, it does not appear as if the courts' bail decisions are influenced by the decision-making of the police. This finding is complicated, however, by the apparent custom and practice of the court routinely to apply bail conditions in the majority of cases.

Seriousness of offence

The seriousness of the offence was the most cited reason for magistrates' bail decisions. As previously noted, however, the courts did not appear to use offence seriousness in bail decisions as they are required to in sentencing decisions. Thus the court does not have to be satisfied that the offence is so serious that only a remand in custody is justified. To explore this issue further the range of offences found for the sample of defendants has been collapsed into three categories: property offences (criminal damage, burglary, theft, handling stolen goods and going equipped), violent offences (ABH, threatening behaviour and harassment), and serious violent offences (robbery, GBH and affray). These offence categories have been mapped against court bail decisions – as shown in table 4.9.

Table 4.9 Offence seriousness by magistrates' bail decision

	Remanded in custody	Conditional bail	Conditional bail (routine conditions)	Unconditional bail
Property offences	10 (7.7%)	17 (13.1%)	23 (17.7%)	5 (3.8%)
Serious violent offences	4 (3.1%)	1 (0.8%)	4 (3.1%)	0
Violent offences	5 (3.8%)	6 (4.6%)	47 (36.2%)	4 (3.1%)

These findings suggest a mixed pattern of behaviour. Those defendants charged with serious violent offences were denied unconditional bail – suggesting at least a partial link between the seriousness of the offence and bail outcomes (although the relevant sample size is very small and further study would be needed to confirm this suggestion). No such pattern is discernible in respect of violent offences, however. Most defendants charged with violent offences were given bail with routine conditions – the majority of these (N=38) being charged with ABH. Four out of five defendants charged with a violent offence and remanded in custody were charged with 'harassment'.

A greater proportion of property offenders were remanded in custody or made subject to specific bail conditions, than those charged with violent offences. On the information available from court records it is not possible fully to account for these patterns of decision-making. It may be that the circumstances surrounding the commission of violent and property offences are different enough to make the denial of unconditional bail and the imposition of conditions 'make sense'; for example the likelihood of offending on bail for property offenders may be reduced if tighter bail conditions are imposed. Further research is necessary before an answer can be given to this question. Alternatively, there may be offender characteristics (for example, previous patterns of behaviour, previous offending, an association between drugs and alcohol and offending, and so on) which distinguish between violent and property offenders – which in turn shapes the type of bail decisions made.

To explore this issue a little further the reasons magistrates gave for their bail decisions was broken down for the different offence types. In practice it was common to find magistrates giving up to three reasons for their bail decision (in 24 cases two reasons were given and in six cases three reasons were given). These variations in practice were not the primary focus of this research and for present purposes reference has been made only to the main or first given reason for the bail decision.

Table 4.10 Offence seriousness by magistrates' main reason for bail decision

	Fail to appear	Previous conduct on bail	Commit further offences	Interfere with witnesses	Seriousness of offence	No bail conditions	No reason given
Serious violent offences	1 (0.8%)	1 (0.8%)	3 (2.3%)	2 (1.5%)	1 (0.8%)	0	1 (0.8%)
Violent offences	4 (3.1%)	0	6 (4.6%)	11 (8.5%)	25 (19.2%)	4 (3.1%)	12 (9.2%)
Property offences	4 (3.1%)	8 (6.2%)	11 (8.5%)	0	17 (13.1%)	5 (3.8%)	10 (7.7%)

These data necessitate a reassessment of the previous discussion. First of all, with respect to defendants charged with serious violent offences, the data show that magistrates only cited 'seriousness of offence' as the main reason for their bail decision in one case. These findings suggest, therefore, that as far as bail decisions are concerned, the seriousness of the offence does not have the same impact as it does in reaching sentencing decisions. Under these circumstances it is reasonable to expect, therefore, that a number of offender characteristics are important factors in influencing bail decisions. If this were the case, we should find a larger number of cases where 'failure to appear', 'previous conduct on bail', and/or 'likely to commit further offences' are cited as the main reason for refusal of bail. In fact, as table 4.10 shows, this was not the case as 'seriousness of offence' predominates as the reason magistrates have given for their bail decisions.

The picture that emerges from these findings is a rather confused one; at least it is not fully explained by the available information. In practice it is probably the case that one, or a combination of the following is happening:

- Magistrates' decision-making is idiosyncratic, and 'seriousness of offence' is being used to justify the denial of unconditional bail as the definition of seriousness is flexible enough to justify almost any decision.
- Magistrates are making decisions in the absence of good-quality, robust offender information and are less able to cite relevant factors as reasons for their bail decisions.
- Magistrates are 'playing safe' in denying unconditional bail to the vast majority of defendants.
- There are factors which the courts have no option but to take into account in making their bail decisions (for example, where a defendant is homeless), but which are not reflected in the Bail Act 1976 (as amended) thereby causing magistrates to rely on other formal justifications for their decisions.

Apart from the fact that magistrates appeared routinely to attach bail conditions to the majority of defendants, these findings do not present a picture of bail decisions overly rigid or determined by single factors. Notwithstanding the above caveat, it appears as though cases are assessed according to their own merits, on the basis of the information available to the court, and that courts can and do take into account a range of information concerning: the seriousness of the offence, the circumstances of the offence, the circumstances and characteristics of the defendant, and other information put before the court concerning the defendant's likely future behaviour on bail (see also Morgan and Henderson 1998; Raine and Willson 1996).

Final main sentence

Probation Service court officers often remark that magistrates may use a custodial remand to give a defendant a 'taste of custody' even where they are not thinking in terms of a custodial sentence. The veracity of this belief has not been fully tested here or elsewhere. In any attempt to gauge the potential impact of pre-trial services on bail decision-making, however, it is instructive to explore these decisions in the light of final sentencing outcomes.

Table 4.11 Sentence by magistrates' bail decision

	Remand in custody	Conditional bail	Conditional bail (routine conditions)	Unconditional bail
Custody	6 (4.6%)	6 (4.6%)	4 (3.1%)	0
Combination order	0	3 (2.3%)	3 (2.3%)	0
Community service order	1 (0.8%)	2 (1.5%)	3 (2.3%)	1 (0.8%)
Probation order	4 (3.1%)	8 (6.2%)	17 (13.1%)	1 (0.8%)
Fine	0	3 (2.3%)	6 (4.6%)	3 (2.3%)
Compensation order	0	0	4 (3.1%)	0
Conditional discharge	0	1 (0.8%)	12 (9.2%)	1 (0.8%)
Case dismissed or withdrawn	8 (6.2%)	2 (1.5%)	28 (21.5%)	3 (2.3%)

It has already been argued that bail decisions and sentencing decisions are separate and distinct in two main ways: (i) they occur at different points in the criminal justice process, and (ii) the factors relevant to decision-making at these different points are themselves weighed differently. Any attempt to explore the relationship between bail and sentencing decisions must be undertaken in the context of this finding, and, in the current exercise, any conclusions that may be drawn must be seen as tentative and in need of further, more explicit, attention. Bearing these points in mind, a number of features emerge from the data in table 4.11.

It is far from clear that there is any kind of relationship between custodial remands and custodial sentences. Only one-third of defendants remanded in custody actually received a custodial sentence; five defendants ultimately received a community sentence, but the largest number (eight defendants) had their cases either withdrawn or discontinued. Whether these findings suggest that magistrates make a pre-emptive strike with a custodial remand cannot be substantiated on the basis of the available information, but the data do raise some important questions:

- How can the courts remand in custody such a high proportion of defendants where the case against them is so weak as to be ultimately withdrawn or discontinued?
- Why have no defendants who were remanded in custody been made subject to a combination order, when this is the primary strategic alternative to custody sentence?
- What factors lead courts to a custodial remand, but ultimately to a community sentence?

At the other end of the sentencing tariff, the findings from this study show that 20 per cent of defendants denied unconditional bail ultimately received a financial penalty. Three-quarters of these defendants were made subject to what we have called 'routine bail conditions'. Notwithstanding the differences in the relevance of factors associated with bail and sentencing decisions, the validity or necessity of the imposition of bail conditions for defendants in this category must be questioned. There is, of course, a question mark over the legality of these decisions to impose routine bail conditions (see also Raine and Willson 1996), but one must ask whether the denial of unconditional bail would have been necessary if the court had more and better-quality information on which to base its decision.

Finally, it is important to pay some attention to community sentences and bail decisions. The majority of defendants finally sentenced to a community sentence were denied unconditional bail. Most of these defendants (N=23) were actually made subject to what we have called 'routine bail conditions', and only 13 (10 per cent of the total population) were made subject to more specific conditions. What these findings suggest is that there is no obvious link between bail decisions, and in particular the conditions that are imposed on defendants on bail, and community sentences. This reinforces the conclusion made previously that bail decisions and sentencing decisions are separate and distinct, but it does raise the question whether this should be the case – at least as far as the application of specific bail conditions and ultimate community sentences are concerned. If at the bail stage the court is concerned about certain offender characteristics so that it feels it necessary to impose specific conditions to bail, then might it not be reasonable to expect these factors to be relevant also at the sentencing stage? The lack of a relationship between the denial of unconditional bail and the imposition of community sentences suggests that court services and court decision-making are poorly targeted and that the system is not joined up in a comprehensive or cohesive manner, but more characterized by *ad hoc* and isolated decision-making. Overall, therefore, there does not appear to be any relationship between bail decisions and final sentencing outcomes.

Bail: a neglected decision?

Although this study was not primarily concerned with an analysis of bail decision-making, it has been necessary to explore this area of the criminal justice system in order to expose the potential for targeted remand services to reduce the number of defendants remanded in custody. Before this issue is explicitly addressed, this study has afforded the opportunity to draw some observations about the bail decision and court practice. These issues are raised in the context of the bail decision as a neglected area of criminal justice decision-making and of criminological inquiry. A review of the literature uncovered very few recent research studies which focused explicitly on the subject of bail (see Raine and Willson 1996; Hucklesby 1997a, 1997b, although Home Office research has focused on the impact on bail decisions of particular programmes, for which see, for example, Morgan and Henderson 1998).

This research has focused explicitly on bail decision-making. In this study we set out to collect comprehensive information about magistrates' use of unconditional bail, conditional bail and cus-todial remands – including information concerning the offence and offender factors which influenced bail outcomes. We have noted that the study was based on court records and that in order to collect fully comprehensive information a 'real time' study is needed; nevertheless this research made a serious attempt to collect the relevant data from court records and found that these records were seriously deficient in the following ways:

- Sentencing data were computerized, but court processing information was held separately in paper files. There was no comprehensive or coherent record system in place.
- Building paper files was an administrative process. The files were not routinely consulted and there was no attempt to analyse or do anything with the information that was collected. Thus many files were found to contain missing papers and it was frequently found that papers were incomplete. For example, in the majority of cases information concerning defendants' previous convictions was missing from the court records.
- There was no record in the court files of the sex of the defendant, and this information could not be obtained or verified from any other source.
- There was no record in the court files of the ethnic origin of the defendant, and this information could not be obtained or verified from any other source.
- The court files did not contain any record of the offender characteristics which may have been relevant to the bail decision (following the Bail Act 1976), or any account of the factors taken into account by magistrates in their decision-making, or any assessment of the value magistrates placed on particular pieces of information. In other words, there was no accurate account of the magistrates' decision or of the process by which the decision was made.
- There was no record in the court files of any additional factors, such as the defendant's housing situation, which are widely known to affect bail decisions.

Several key findings about the bail decision have, however, been uncovered by this research:

- Bail decisions are particular and specific. The factors which appear to be relevant to the bail decision are distinct from those associated with sentencing practices.
- The reasons given for bail decisions are not outcome-specific. In other words, magistrates give the same reasons for denial of unconditional bail as they do for denial of bail.
- Within the criminal justice process, from arrest to sentence, a series of

decisions must be taken to move defendants through the legal system. These decisions, including the bail decision, appear to be taken in an isolated manner – each decision is made sequentially and separately as defendants pass through the criminal justice process. There is no individual or agency seeking to ensure any overall coherence to the criminal justice process.

- Magistrates' bail decision-making does not appear to be influenced by any single offence or offender characteristic, nor does it appear to follow any particular custom (except the application of routine conditions), or to be fixed or predetermined. In other words, magistrates do not appear to make bail decisions in an actuarial manner, or on the basis of particular categories of offences or offender characteristics; rather, bail decisions appear to be individualized.

- Notwithstanding the above, the courts appear to apply basic conditions to bail in an apparently routine manner in a large number of cases, thereby raising questions as to the legality of many bail decisions. This suggests that magistrates' decision-making is most powerfully influenced by a local court culture (or custom, Hucklesby 1997b) and possibly a notion of 'safety-first'. Thus bail decisions are only individualized within the paradigm of court culture and it is this which shapes court behaviour more than the personal characteristics or charges faced by the defendant.

- There appear to be, at best, only tenuous links between the offence and offender characteristics which influence the bail decision, and the reasons magistrates give for these decisions. In particular there is an over-reliance on 'seriousness of the offence' as the main reason for particular bail decisions, but no apparent relationship between the seriousness of the offence and the bail decision. This finding reflects the poor quality of the Bail Act 1976 and the *ad hoc* nature in which this area of legislation has been developed.

These findings lead to the conclusion that bail has been a neglected area of the criminal justice system and as a result it is a part of the system which has become confused and overgrown. There is a lack of coherence to the law on bail, there is a lack of coherence to the practice of bail decision-making, there is an absence of oversight of bail decision-making, there is an absence of any individual or agency taking responsibility for bail and for managing its place within the criminal justice system, and there is a lack of information and hence understanding of this crucial part of the criminal process.

The potential scope for pre-trial services

The aim of this final section is to explore the potential contribution to a reduction in the remand population that may be achieved by an effective remand management strategy. The extent to which this analysis can be achieved is limited by the information that was available from court records. In practice, for a remand management strategy to be effective the services offered by the Probation Service must address the objections to bail or the factors that concern the court which lead to a denial of bail. These factors include both offence and offender characteristics. Offence factors mostly concern the seriousness of the offence (which, as the above analysis has shown, is a malleable concept), but offender characteristics comprise a much larger set of factors. Some of these factors are delineated in the Bail Act 1976, for example the number and type of previous convictions, the defendant's previous behaviour and conduct on bail. There are, however, a range of additional offender characteristics which influence the bail decision, for example the offender's housing situation, whether the offence is associated with drugs or alcohol, the stability (or otherwise) of the offender's social situation, the attitude of the offender towards the offence, the attitude and relationship of the offender (if any) to the victim, employment status and (as far as it is relevant and known to the court) the offender's previous response to community sentences. To evaluate the ability and extent to which the Probation Service can address these factors, and thus reduce unnecessary custodial remands, it is essential that the full range of offender characteristics is known and quantified. These data, however, are not available from court records (or any other existing local information system), and therefore outside the scope of this analysis. Further research is urgently required to fill this gap in the present knowledge, and for current purposes we are limited to undertaking a more general assessment of the potential impact of pre-trial services on the bail process.

Systems management

Bail decisions are amongst the most important actions that magistrates must take. The decision to grant bail (even with restrictions) must balance the risk to the public presented by continued liberty with the seriousness of depriving an individual of freedom. This decision has to be taken in the context that the criminal justice system is based on the principles of justice and fairness, and balancing this range of (often competing) concerns is a complex and difficult task. Yet courts are required to make these decisions in far from ideal circumstances. Bail decisions are made at the earliest stages of the criminal justice process, when the amount of information available to the court, on which to base its decision, is frequently very limited. Furthermore, what information is available is presented to the court either by the prosecution alone (as many defendants are not legally represented at these early stages) or by the prosecution and the defence. The presentation of information by these parties is, therefore, naturally slanted towards the objectives of either side in an adversarial system. Under these circumstances the court is forced to make its own assessment of the veracity of this information, without the benefit of reliable and robust impartial information of its own. It is not surprising that such a dysfunctional system leads to poor-quality decision-making.

Like sentencing decisions, bail decisions are broadly individualized; in other words each decision is made on the basis of an assessment of the factors associated with each individual. Individualism as a sentencing principle was firmly established by the Criminal Justice Act 1991, and although in recent years there has been a move towards an increasingly actuarial decision (based on the score an individual achieves on standard risk assessment tools), the process of sentencing relies heavily on the provision of information to the court. Thus information is central to the operation of modern court systems. To meet the demands for information modern criminal justice systems have established a specialist agency to fulfil this role. In some continental systems this role is the responsibility of specially appointed examining magistrates, but in most systems it is fulfilled by the Probation Service.

In England and Wales, as far as the bail decision is concerned, this chapter (see also Haines and Octigan 1999) has shown that the system is not information-rich. Moreover this chapter has shown that the pre-trial process has been somewhat neglected and allowed to become overgrown and unmanaged. In general the amount and quality of local and national information about bail decisions is very poor. The Prison Service and the Home Office monitor the number of custodial remands, and the Lord Chancellor's Department (through its Time Interval Surveys, see LCD 1999) monitors the average time taken from offence through to completion of the criminal process, but information about the reasons for remand decisions, the use of conditional bail and why cases take the amount of time they do is not available.

There is an urgent need, therefore, for a proactive bail management strategy. In itself this is not an argument for the Probation Service to provide an enhanced bail information service, although bail information would comprise an important part of this strategy. Bail information services, in the manner in which they have been developed hitherto, have not been conceived as part of a connected systems management strategy, but in a more isolated manner as providing information to improve the quality of one decision without a view as to the consequences of this. In contrast a bail management strategy would begin by mapping and quantifying the throughput of local courts. Monitoring systems would be developed to aggregate decision-making for the whole of the pre-trial process, and to collect information on the reasons and outcomes of all decisions. On the basis of this information it would be possible to identify key decision-making points within the system and to identify the factors on which decisions are made. Good-quality information would also highlight why particular decisions are being made, and would allow probation services to develop strategies and services to target change in these decisions in line with agreed local and national policies.

Taking a systems management approach to the delivery of remand services has a number of advantages:

- Getting the system right is more efficient and effective than continual individual problem solving.
- Decisions made early on in the system affect the sequence of decision-making from these early points of intervention. An otherwise 'high-risk' defendant who successfully completes a bail support package is placed in a better position to receive a community sentence than someone remanded in custody.
- Decision-making over time can be influenced, that is, successful unconditional bail for one offence can influence future decision-making should the same person be subsequently charged with another offence.
- Overall decision-making can be improved, and costly but unnecessary use of custody can be avoided.
- Overall system behaviour is more readily amenable to strategic change

as a series of, for example, successful unconditional bail decisions can inform and influence future decisions in this direction.

At the present time, national and local policies and objectives for bail do not exist in any meaningful form, as the information required to develop these policies is simply not available. The potential scope for remand services to have a significant impact on the bail process is dependent upon the routine production of good-quality, robust information – backed up by effective services. The development of national and local policies for bail, and the development of remand services is thus contingent upon the development of a proactive bail management strategy.

Targeting conditional bail

A proactive bail management strategy would not focus on one part of the bail process (for example enhancing bail information or reducing custodial remands), but would be concerned with the whole of the bail process. A pivotal target within such a strategy would be conditional bail, and such a strategy would comprise a number of distinct elements.

The Bail Act 1976 enshrines the right to unconditional bail, which may only be denied if certain specific conditions are met. As this study has shown, there appears to be what may, at best, be interpreted as a fairly loose application of the Bail Act in the large-scale denial of unconditional bail to over 90 per cent of defendants and the granting of conditional bail with what we have termed 'routine conditions' in 59.2 per cent of cases. This finding, and the extent to which this practice was commonplace within the large metropolitan court in this study, represents practices which were clearly never intended in the Bail Act 1976 and which may actually comprise routine miscarriages of justice (see also Raine and Willson 1996).

To be sure, a proportion of decisions to grant defendants conditional bail with 'routine conditions' will be justified. On the basis of information available in court case files, it was not possible to estimate what this proportion was. But the application of routine conditions was such a widespread practice as to raise important concerns about the legality of the courts' decision-making. A necessary component of a proactive bail management strategy would, therefore, be improving the quality and legality of bail decisions. Key elements of a proactive bail management strategy in this respect would be: (i) monitoring and information systems designed to detect such practices, (ii) the provision of offender information to improve the quality of bail decision-making, and (iii) monitoring the outcome of bail decisions to ensure the development of professional knowledge of the effectiveness of decision-making. Current practice in the area of bail is unmonitored, and there is a lack of accountability for decision-making and an absence of any agency taking responsibility for what happens to defendants during this stage of the criminal justice process. A proactive bail management strategy would be designed to remedy this shortfall.

Beyond issues of justice and strictly legal concerns, the ability of the courts to attach conditions to bail is of immense strategic and practice significance. If the court is to be enabled to avoid a custodial remand where the offence and offender characteristics make denial of bail a possibility, it must be given good reasons to do so. As we have noted, courts may only deny unconditional bail if the offence or offences a defendant is charged with are serious enough or if there is evidence in the defendant's antecedents or previous behaviour that give the court good reason to believe that the defendant may commit further offences on bail, fail to appear at a future specified court date, or interfere with witnesses. Beyond the arguments and assurances of defence solicitors, the Probation Service is the only organization that is capable of developing a strategy to target the bail decision, of providing information and services that directly address objections to bail and of developing the confidence of the court. Indeed, there is ample precedent for the ability of a community-based justice agency to carry out this role in the youth court effectively (Haines and Drakeford 1998).

Targeting custodial remands

A key performance indicator for a proactive bail management strategy would be the ability of the service to reduce the number of unnecessary or inappropriate custodial remands. There will always be defendants for whom anything but a remand in custody is untenable; the offences, previous record and behaviour of some defendants present a serious and ongoing risk to the public, and such defendants (who are likely, in any case, to receive a custodial sentence) will continue to be remanded in custody. A proactive bail management strategy must be properly and effectively targeted. But as this study has shown, a significant proportion of defendants are seemingly remanded in custody unnecessarily, and there is, at present, no mechanism or system of assessment which permits an evaluation of whether those defendants who are currently remanded in custody should be there.

A surprising finding of this research was the high number of cases that were ultimately discontinued or withdrawn. In the sample as a whole, which was randomly drawn from a year of court throughput, 31.5 per cent of cases were either discontinued or withdrawn (Home Office figures show a national rate of 22 per cent, which is still very high, Harries 1999). The court in this study dealt with approximately 14,000 adult cases per year (excluding motoring offences and cases remitted to the Crown Court); thus approximately 4,500 defendants were ultimately not proceeded against. Within the sample of cases we examined, nineteen (14.7 per cent) were remanded in custody. Eight of these defendants (42.1 per cent) had their cases either discontinued or withdrawn. As the sample of court cases was drawn randomly it is reasonable to assume that the selected cases are representative of overall court behaviour. This suggests that of the 14,000 cases dealt with per year, just over 2,000 defendants are remanded in custody but approximately 850 of these defendants are not proceeded against.

To be sure, the decision to discontinue or withdraw a case is mainly a matter for the court and the Crown Prosecution Service, but this is not the whole story. One of the main objectives of a proactive bail management strategy is an overall improvement of the quality of pre-sentence decision-making. It is about the taking of responsibility for this area of criminal justice decision-making and raising the standards of justice achieved in this area. As such, it is legitimate to expect, in general terms, a proactive bail management strategy to have a significant impact on all areas of bail decision-making, including those cases which are ultimately discontinued or withdrawn. It is, however, possible to do more.

Motivated by concerns about the level of offending on bail, the Home Office initiated the bail process project in five court areas in 1993 (Morgan and Henderson 1998). The bail process project was essentially concerned to improve the amount and quality of information available to the court to enable more informed (and hence better) bail decisions. To facilitate increased information flow the project was designed as an inter-agency structure, bringing together court staff, the CPS, the police and the Probation Service. As the inter-agency steering group in each of the five areas had a degree of autonomy in how the project developed, the schemes varied in nature and activity. Overall, the results of the project on offending on bail were mixed, but all projects were characterized (to varying degrees) by their attempts to gain some control over the bail process. These efforts did not seek to control decision-making or outcomes, but were targeted at improving the quality of the court process. While the project demonstrated some success in this respect, mostly (it appears) as a result of particular initiatives taken by a key local individual, overall the gains were disappointing and not sustained.

The apparent failure of the bail process project can be attributed to two key factors:

- The objectives for the project (reducing offending on bail) were probably too ambitious and too narrowly drawn. Had the projects been directed at improving the flow of information, clearer means of achieving this objective could have been articulated.
- The structure of the project was not well suited to achieving the given objectives or to improving the quality of decision-making pre-sentence. There was a lack of clarity in the model itself regarding working methods and so on, but also a lack of clear leadership and lines of authority and responsibility for making the project work.

A poorly designed project, therefore, produced poor results. A project with much clearer objectives and methods was initiated at about the same time. The Public Interest Case Assessment project was designed to improve the amount and quality of information made available to the Crown Prosecution Service to enable a fuller assessment, as part of the legal responsibility of the CPS to review cases, of whether prosecution was necessary in the public interest.

These projects reinforce the conclusions made here that the whole area of bail decision-making is a neglected criminal justice backwater which is desperately in need of sustained attention and improvement. These isolated projects have shown that bail decisions can be targeted and that cases discontinued or withdrawn can be addressed in these targeting exercises. A Probation Service proactive bail management strategy can address the very significant area of cases which are discontinued or withdrawn if the strategy is comprehensively drawn. If such a strategy were to be implemented in a wholly effective manner, in one year this could have reduced the number of defendants remanded in custody in the one court involved in this study by 850. Even if a more realistic target were 50 per cent of this number, this would still have reduced the remand population by 425.

Another important target in a comprehensive bail management strategy is that group of defendants who are currently remanded in custody but who ultimately receive a community sentence. Despite the number of Home Office-initiated bail-related projects that have been tried since the early 1990s, there appears to be an institutional reluctance on the part of the Probation Service to engage in this work (Haines and Octigan 1999). To be sure, the failure to learn from and capitalize on these experiences cannot solely be laid at the door of the Probation Service, but there is a conceptual wall within probation thinking which has prevented the service from engaging with the challenges and opportunities that arise before pre-sentence inquiries are made. The strong tradition within mainstream probation practice and management that the service does not actively engage itself within the system or with offenders until a finding of guilt (and a request for a pre-sentence report has been made) severely limits the potential for the service to have an effective impact on sentencing.

In this study we found that 26.3 per cent of defendants who were remanded in custody were ultimately made subject to a community sentence (compared to 22 per cent of those granted unconditional bail, 30 per cent of those on routine bail conditions and 52 per cent of those on specific bail conditions). Whilst this study cannot shed any light on the effectiveness of the targeting of community sentences (in terms of offence or offender characteristics), these figures at least suggest that:

- Properly targeted bail support services could reduce the number of custodial remands by up to one-quarter.
- If the mainstream Probation Service were more actively engaged in the criminal justice process before sentencing then not only could the court be made aware of the suitability of this 26.3 per cent of defendants for a community sentence, but this proportion could be increased.

If the Probation Service is able to demonstrate that a defendant can comply with a period of supervised bail and if, as a result, the service is better able to make an assessment of the likely impact of a community sentence and thus better able to articulate the contents and purpose of such a sentence (based on direct experience) then it is much more difficult for the court ultimately to impose a custodial sentence. This is a significant gain in itself, but one should not ignore the possibilities such practice will gain in terms of the improved effectiveness of community sentences themselves.

Moving to such a model of practice will require not only training, but a re-articulation of the basis of probation thinking. It is perhaps not surprising that this study found that none of those defendants remanded in custody were ultimately made subject to a combination order – despite the fact that this community sentence is the main high tariff alternative to custody, as this anomaly is in fact indicative of current mainstream probation thinking and practice, and symptomatic of the reluctance of the service to engage the system and offenders pre-sentence. In one year a proactive bail management strategy targeted on the bail or jail decision, that was limited only to those defendants who ultimately received a community sentence, could have reduced the remand population by about 500 in one magistrates' court.

It is important to take care in not setting unrealistic targets or expectations for a bail management strategy. The bail decision is not the same as the sentencing decision. As we have shown above, different factors weigh on the courts at these different decision-making points. There may be good reasons for this (for example, the likelihood of a defendant interfering with witnesses and perverting the course of justice), but the level of disjunction and apparent discontinuity between the bail and sentencing decisions is a matter worthy of further attention. Ultimately it will be for Parliament to resolve the legal inconsistencies in bail legislation and to bring to the bail decision the mechanisms and tools (such as risk assessment) currently utilized in sentencing decisions. There is much, however, that can be achieved within the current system.

If one takes a comprehensive systems approach to understanding court processes (which, as we have argued, is essential for an effective proactive bail management strategy) new perspectives and opportunities emerge. Tackling the number of unnecessary or inappropriate custodial remands, therefore, is not simply about targeting the 'bail or jail' decision (although this will remain an important aspect of the strategy). The systems perspective alerts us to the importance of tackling the sequence of decisions that ultimately leads to a custodial remand. This study and Hucklesby (1997b) have shown how bail decision-making is heavily influenced by court culture, custom and practice. This study has also shown how bail decisions are individualized and malleable. Change within the system is, therefore, possible. The key to reducing the number of unnecessary and inappropriate custodial remands lies, therefore, as much in improving court decision-making, tightening the application of the Bail Act 1976, increasing the use of unconditional bail and more effectively targeted use of conditional bail as it does in targeting the bail or jail decision itself. Based on the limited figures available from this study, and using a conservative estimate of the level of effectiveness, one could legitimately expect a proactive bail management strategy to reduce the custodial remand population by about 50 per cent. In the one court in which this study took place, this would mean approximately 1,000 fewer defendants remanded in custody in a year.

National gains

What national gains might be legitimately expected from an effective proactive bail management strategy? If we assume, for the moment, that the behaviour of the court in this study is representative of magistrates' courts nationally, then it is possible to make some estimates.

Home Office statistics show that in 1998 there were about 132,100 sentenced receptions into custody, and that 52 per cent of these were previously held on remand (White 1999). There were thus approximately 60,000 defendants remanded in custody in England and Wales in 1998. If a proactive bail management strategy were in place nationally and operating at the level of effectiveness suggested above, then we could legitimately expect this strategy to reduce the number of defendants remanded in custody by about 30,000 to a level of 30,000 defendants per year.

Remand prisoners, of course, do not normally spend more than a few weeks in custody. Thus the average daily population of remand prisoners is about 12,000 (of whom two-thirds are unsentenced) (White and Woodbridge 1998). A fully effective national pro-active bail management strategy might, therefore, be expected to reduce the average daily prison population by about 6,000.

It is difficult to obtain accurate and robust costs on the operation of the criminal justice system. Based on Home Office estimates (Harries 1999) the average cost of a remand prisoner is £5,000. Based on personal communications with the Home Office we can assume this figure is an underestimate as it includes: (i) an estimate of court costs, plus (ii) an estimate of Prison Service costs, but it does not include the costs of transportation or holding defendants in police cells (and incidentals such as meals). Nevertheless, £5,000 is the best available estimate of the average cost of a remand, and working with this figure an estimate of the total cost of the remand population is £300,000,000 (about 3 per cent of an estimate of the costs of the criminal justice system). A comprehensive effective pro-active bail management strategy might, therefore, be expected to save £150 million per year at current rates and costs.

These figures are, of course, tentative; and the costs do not take account of the resources needed to deploy a national proactive bail management strategy (although these are likely to be relatively small compared with the costs of remand – the whole of the Probation Service costs about £600 million). Nevertheless, these figures demonstrate that there are considerable human, legal, social and financial benefits to be derived from the operational-ization of an effective bail management strategy.

Conclusion

This chapter set out to explore the impact on the remand population of a proactive remand management strategy. As a result of undertaking this analysis a broader objective has emerged, that of exploring the potential of a proactive bail management strategy.

The necessity of widening the scope of a remand management strategy into a bail management strategy is derived from the findings that the whole area of bail decision-making is much neglected and redolent of poor practice. There is thus an overriding need for an agency to get to grips with bail and to take responsibility for managing this aspect of criminal justice practice, and for improving the quality of justice and practice in the area of bail.

5. Probation Prospects and Pre-trial Services: A View from the Bridge

Introduction

This is not a book which espouses a 'great woman', or even a 'great man' approach to history or the making of social policy. Nevertheless, in researching the contemporary state of the Probation Service and its preparedness to take on new duties in the field of pre-trial services, it seemed important, at a time of rapid change, to attempt to capture the views and the voices of those major players and interest groups who are influential in shaping the climate of present-day practice and in producing the practical response to policy developments. The connection between the findings presented in this chapter and the role of probation in the pre-trial process is a direct, but crucial one. In other parts of this book we have sought to establish the case for the more central involvement of the probation service in pre-trial services. The practical possibility of achieving such a shift, however, depends not simply upon the strength of the case made, but upon the culture of the service in which change is to be brought about and the views and dispositions of those upon whom the responsibility for initiating and implementing change would fall. This chapter aims to explore these contextual issues, by recording and exploring the views of some key actors. Of course, such views and voices are only particular strands in the complex web through which practical alteration is brought about in the approach to, and the delivery of, services. The individuals reported here are all, to differing degrees, insiders in the probation world. While most will have risen through the ranks of field workers and middle management, all today occupy positions of greater prominence within their own immediate workplaces and the wider stage upon which probation issues are discussed and debated.

While the selection of the individuals whose views are reported here can make no claim to scientific representativeness, the names which emerged were the product of a careful selection process. The list was compiled by those engaged in, and overseeing, the research project on the basis of informed knowledge and the wish to obtain a range of relevant interests and perspectives. Final decisions were shaped, additionally, by considerations of race and gender. A schedule of questions was posed at each interview in order to explore a common curriculum of core concerns. It is important to stress that no respondent interviewed was either asked or claimed to 'represent' any viewpoint other than their own. While speaking in a personal capacity, however, respondents clearly reflect the perspective which their particular engagement in and with the probation world provides.

Leadership and the probation service

Before proceeding to the interviews themselves, a couple of pieces of contextualization need to be put in place, in order to aid understanding of the views reported here. The individuals interviewed are drawn from what might broadly be called the 'leadership' of the Probation Service. In the language of the last two decades of the twentieth century, the majority would be most closely identified with its 'management' class. It is important, therefore, briefly to locate the notions of leadership and management in the service within those wider debates about its purpose and direction which have characterized probation discussions for over a quarter of a century.

The rise of managerialism in the public services has been extensively documented, particularly in relation to the 'New Public Management' approaches of the neo-liberal reforms of the Thatcher era. Coming to prominence in the later years of the 1970s, this approach was highly critical of the traditional management styles which it claimed prevailed in the public services since the foundation of the welfare state. In essence, these previous approaches were said to have been unresponsive and bureaucratic in dealing with the public, expansionist and status-seeking in relation to other public services, and diplomatic to the point of appeasement in dealing with staffing and industrial relations matters (see Drakeford 1999). In their place, this analysis suggested, should be developed a new approach to management within the public sector which would be active rather than passive, determined in its pursuit of businesslike methods, attuned to the demands of leanness and efficiency, accountable to users rather than providers of services, and confident in its own right to manage.

Such a powerful general thrust within the public services inevitably produced an impact upon the Probation Service. Vanstone (1988) has written persuasively about the pitfalls which lay in wait for those who attempted to translate the new imperatives directly into a context which, at that time at least, drew its prevailing ethos from the values of co-operation and reconciliation. The rise of managerialism threatened to create a widening gap between 'headquarters management and the staff engaged in the core tasks of the agency' (Raynor et al. 1994: 139) which, at its worst, appeared to cope with the demands of accountancy and accountability by a retreat to a sort of macho management-by-orders.

Nor were concerns about the changing nature of management confined to the internal workings of the service. From the election of 1979 onwards, the progressive politicization of criminal justice matters shone a persistent spotlight upon the place of the Probation Service in the new era. Some of the changes which followed were welcomed by important service interests. The general protection offered to law and order services was extended to probation and, as a result, it found itself sheltered from the cutbacks in expenditure which were characteristic of other public services. The claims by government to be moving probation 'centre stage' in the lead-up to the 1991 Criminal Justice Act were also considered by some influential commentators (Ashworth et al. 1992; Shaw and Haines 1989) to be worth the price which was extracted in terms of the new language to be applied to its activities, with its emphasis on *punishment* in the community and new national standards of *enforcement*. In this relatively optimistic analysis, Probation Service leadership had shown itself to be quietly skilful in adapting to the form, if not the content, of the new demands placed upon it, retaining the essential and distinctive character of the probation enterprise, taking advantage of the opportunities which the changed climate brought with it, while avoiding its dangers.

Against these more optimistic voices, a second strand remained more critical of the leadership of the service, suggesting that its strategy of accommodation to the regularly changing demands of the Home Office left a vacuum at the heart of the service itself. At best, it might be argued from this perspective, probation leadership lacked confidence in the qualities of the service it led or the courage to defend these qualities when they came under attack. At worst, it could be suggested, senior managers in the service were actively engaged in the embrace of an agenda driven not by evolutionary change but by the wholesale transformation of an essentially socially democratic, European social work service, into the correctional cadres of the American model.

The purpose of this brief excursion into the contested history of the modern Probation Service, and the role of senior figures within it, is to make clear the context within which the views to which this chapter now turns were elicited. The ground is uncertain beneath the feet of anyone seeking to look, as our respondents were asked, from the present to the future. Both in terms of their own immediate operating environment, and in terms of the wider world outside, the challenge facing all those with a stake and a say in shaping the future of the Probation Service is considerable.

Limitations

The picture which emerges from this set of perspectives necessarily leaves out a number of other interest groups which are bound to be influential in the operation of any organization. The views of people who appear before the courts, and who are made subject to supervision in different forms by the Probation Service, play no direct part in the discussion which follows. In so far as they enter the calculations of our respondents, they do so relatively unproblematically. As a later section of this chapter will suggest in more detail, the civil liberty arguments, which must form part of any careful consideration of intervention in the lives of citizens prior to a judicial determination of their cases, rest lightly in the minds of most respondents. The benefits for those made subject to such arrangements loom larger for our interviewees than any disadvantages. Pre-trial services, it is generally suggested, represent a less intrusive form of intervention than would otherwise be the case, and are legitimized as a result.

A second group whose views are largely uncaptured in this chapter is that of main-grade probation officers and other services staff whose day-to-day activities are crucial to the practical accomplishment of any organizational objectives and purposes. These voices have, in particular contexts, been recorded in chapter 3. The capacity of front-line workers to hasten or hinder the achievement of goals set by policy-makers is well documented in the personal social services in which probation has its roots (see, for example, Lipsky 1980). Directly in the field of criminal justice, the coalition of sceptical sentencers and sensible practitioners is often credited with the rapid demise of much-vaunted initiatives such as the attachment of negative conditions to orders made under the 1982 Criminal Justice Act (Jarvis et al. 1987). The absence of practitioner voices is thus significant and only partially resolved by the inclusion of an interview with a senior figure in the National Association of Probation Officers. As in the case of service users, the respondents who do make contributions here have a view of practitioners which they are well able to articulate. It is one of the areas which, as this chapter will demonstrate, most powerfully divides the interviewees.

As well as other internal probation voices, the operation of the service demands the active co-operation of other criminal justice organizations. The interviews carried out here were designed to capture a range of these interests through the roles which individual interviewees occupy. Others, such as the Crown Prosecution Service, do not appear directly in this text. In terms of pre-trial services, of course, the interface between organizations is crucial to the success or otherwise of such schemes. Our interviewees all have reflections to offer upon these boundary issues, especially in the area of finance, as a later section demonstrates. More generally, however, in terms of relations with other bodies, interviewees anticipate relatively few problems in their dealings with outsiders. Of course, in the majority of cases, the individuals whose views are reported here have spent the whole of their working lives inside the Probation Service. Some interesting contrasts emerge, as outlined below, when considering the views of those beyond its own boundaries.

Finally, in this brief review of the limitations which have to be attached to the views reported here, the chapter deals only tangentially with an interest group which has come to be arguably the most powerful and influential within the whole system – that of the politicians. In the interview with the chief inspector of probation, this chapter contains a source which lies close to the motivating concerns of central government. A direct interview with a government minister, however, did not prove possible. In its place, permission was sought, and granted, to use a speech given by the then minister of state at the Home Office, Lord Mostyn, to a special conference, 'Bail or Jail?' held in December 1998, which had as its central concern the development of pre-trial services. The speech covered a great deal of the ground which formed the core of interviews conducted with respondents. It also represents the most authoritative statement of government policy in this field, to date. The speech is used in this chapter in that way, although it inevitably lacks the dialogical character which other contributions display, and did not offer any opportunity for clarification or debate of points raised. From the perspective of those directly interviewed, the increased politicization of the criminal justice system in general, and the role within it of the Probation Service in particular, emerges consistently as a subject of concern and of regret. This chapter will aim to capture some of the context within which that concern has arisen and to trace something of the present government's intentions in relation both to pre-trial services and the future of the service.

If these are some of the limitations which need to be acknowledged in relation to the interviews conducted for this chapter, this section ought not to end without placing proper emphasis upon the positive character of the group whose views are recorded. Outside the directly political sphere, every individual approached in relation to the project freely agreed to participate, and to do so on the terms suggested. The research was therefore able to draw together the views of a range of significant actors from within the sphere of interest under investigation.

The remainder of this chapter reports two essential elements: firstly, it sets out a series of particular aspects of the contemporary probation world upon which those interviewed placed particular weight. This section ends with a summation of the core characteristics which respondents identified as representing the essence of the modern service. Secondly, the chapter goes on to report the attitude of interviewees towards pre-trial services, exploring the part which such services might play in the future of probation and the issues which that future would need to address.

Contemporary probation

Common ground

Given the shared interests of those involved in this project, a substantial degree of common ground between all participants could still be detected in certain key instances. The section which follows aims to isolate, illustrate and discuss these aspects.

A first and striking consistency amongst almost all respondents is the length of time which each has devoted to involvement with the probation service. For the majority, the great bulk of their working lives has been spent directly as employees of the service, working their way from main to chief officer grade. Andrew Underdown, for example, reported: 'I've worked throughout my career for Greater Manchester Probation Service. I have a probation officer background with a wide range of responsibilities. I was a senior probation officer in both field teams and in community service. I've had experience as assistant chief in the operational division covering Oldham and Tameside districts, and for about the last six years I've held the policy and information brief as assistant chief here.' Amongst most respondents this process had occupied many years. Jenny Robert's period of fifteen years as chief officer at Hereford and Worcester had taken her working life in the Probation Service to thirty years. Even those who were no longer directly in the service itself had moved to new duties from lengthy and senior employment within it. Linda Jones, at the time she was interviewed, was seconded to the prison service as an assistant director in charge of a new women's policy group. Her career in the probation service stretched back to 1972, culminating in ten years as chief of the Leicestershire Probation Service. Graham Smith, chief inspector of probation at the time of interview, had, likewise, moved to that post from a mainstream probation career which began in 1965 and included twelve years as chief officer of the Inner London Probation Service.

Only a minority of interviewees in this study failed to conform to this mainstream mould. Two – Cordell Pillay and Helen Schofield – had come to prominence through the National Association of Probation Officers, the organization which, as a professional association and a trade union, represented the interests of the broad range of workers within the service. Neither had worked at chief officer posts within probation, but both had some twenty years as main-grade or senior officer level. At the time of interview, Cordell Pillay remained a nationally elected officer of the National Association of Probation Officers. Helen Schofield had moved at arm's length to the service itself, working since October 1998 in a senior position within the newly established national training organization, responsible for standard setting and occupational development in community services.

A further two interviewees fell outside this pattern of direct, long-term, Probation Service employment. One, Rodney Carroll had, at the time of being interviewed, been the deputy director of the Probation Service employers' organization, the Central Council of Probation Committees, since 1988. Prior to that he had worked as a main-grade probation officer and in social services, becoming the director of the Western Board in Northern Ireland and a member of the original Northern Ireland Probation Board.

What conclusions may be drawn from the pattern of long, senior and consistent service reported here? Firstly, it means that the views represented here are authenticated by experience and by dedication. Secondly, and importantly, there is a danger of insularity. This is a world seen often from inside a rather narrow box. There is some evidence, in the views which follow, of a distinction to be drawn between those who remain insiders, and those whose work has taken them away from the direct world of the service.

A changing world

In order to project a future for the Probation Service it is important to know something of the base from which individuals see that future being shaped. All respondents were asked to identify the main changes which, in their view, had exercised the most important influences over the service during the recent past. While some differences of emphasis were apparent in identifying particular drivers of change, a very real unanimity emerged from all respondents in pointing to the continuous and major nature of change which the service has had to face. In the words of Jenny Roberts, there has been 'massive change', with the service required to make what Linda Jones described as 'huge jumps' in orientation and service delivery. Rodney Carroll put it this way: 'If you were to ask me what the probation service would look like in about ten years' time, I couldn't possibly tell you. Such is the pace of change.'

The following were amongst the most commonly identified characteristics of change.

Money

In discussing the financial circumstances of contemporary probation practice, interviewees focused both upon the amount of money available to the service and the conditions under which funds were spent. The essential context was summed up by Jenny Roberts as 'the ascendancy of the accountants rather than the probation service' and what Helen Schofield called the 'quite extraordinary' impact of changes tied to funding imperatives. Comparing the service Schofield joined in 1975 with that of a quarter of a century later, she traced the financial management initiatives of the early 1980s, with their emphasis on efficiency and effectiveness, the impact of privatization and marketization in the second half of that decade, and the cash-limited retrenchments of the 1990s. In the views of respondents to this study, the financial climate within which the contemporary Probation Service operates provides, at best, a two-edged sword. On the one hand, the emphasis on accountancy is linked, for some, with accountability. In this analysis a present-day robust stewardship of public funds is contrasted with a laxer and less transparent previous regime. On the other hand, and more powerfully, respondents worry about the extent to which financial imperatives have come to be the master rather than the servant of wider service change. From a Home Office perspective, however, the future was described by Graham Smith as one in which 'the issue of value for money is even more important than in the past . . . there is no alternative for the service but to be able to reduce costs and stay equally efficient in providing a quality service'.

The impact of financial constraint upon pre-trial services formed a section in the speech to the 'Bail or Jail?' conference delivered by Lord Mostyn, the minister then responsible for the prison and probation services. He traced the accepted history of these events:

> Let me rehearse some history of the funding of bail information. Originally, money for court-based bail information schemes was provided to probation services specifically for this purpose. That funding was later dehypothecated in the belief that bail information schemes had become embedded as part of normal Probation Service

activity and would continue to be funded if the money specifically earmarked for them was absorbed into the general Probation Service grant. This was a mistake as, when the money was dehypothecated, bail information schemes were run down. (See Haines and Octigan 1999)

Articulating a rather different warning note, Helen Schofield linked the willingness of local probation services to re-engage with such work by suggesting that, 'frankly, now if you put in a penny they'll follow it because they have to'. In other words, while some valuable initiatives come to an end because of funding shortages, other projects may begin simply because money leads them on, rather than because of any genuine commitment to the ideas which such initiatives represent. In either case, the effect is to make the operating environment of such schemes fragile and vulnerable to changes outside their own control.

Politics

Amongst almost all respondents a sense emerged of what Helen Schofield called being 'continually caught in a political arena'. For many respondents, the politicization of criminal justice matters and the fate of the Probation Service in being drawn into this arena were amongst the most significant changes of recent times. Helen Schofield looks back to a time when 'For a long time it was possible to say that politics didn't impact demonstrably on the social services'. More subtly, Graham Smith suggests that an increased political interest in the service during the 1980s was, to some extent, disguised both because a measure of agreement existed between the political parties and, more significantly, because the direction of change brought with it sufficient compensating advantages – chiefly in terms of growth – to be palatable to important interests within the Probation Service. With the advent of Michael Howard, however, the politicization of probation became more starkly revealed, and with it 'cuts in real terms and loss of favour. Those were bad times.' There is a sense in which, having been brought beneath the political spotlight, respondents to this study felt that it could never recapture a sense of prelapsarian innocence again.

Managerialism and autonomy

A common theme, uniting all respondents, drew attention to the rise of managerialism and loss of front-line autonomy within the service. Helen Schofield suggested: 'When I first started, people worked for themselves.' Andrew Underdown described the last fifteen years of probation as a period which had witnessed a 'transformation from the model of a largely autonomous practitioner to a professional working within the management policy framework'. Unsurprisingly, perhaps, given the preponderance of managers amongst those interviewed, the balance of opinion here emphasized the benefits – 'leaner, more efficient, open to greater scrutiny and more competent', thought Graham Smith – which managerialism had brought. Such views were, however, modified by others. Richard Green suggested:

> I suppose the other big change which I referred to earlier is this culture of managerialism which is around and the control from the centre . . . That's good, because in terms of being effective and delivering value for money that's only right, and there is a need for consistency, but I think there is a danger of initiative being lost, of good ideas getting lost, in this drive for consistency.

For many, the tension between autonomy and managerialism was linked to the shift away from other traditional probation values, as the following section suggests.

A social work service?

All interviewees were asked to reflect about the place which the social work inheritance of the service might still have to play in its future operation. It was commonly understood amongst all respondents that government-led changes had shifted the working ethos of the service sharply away from the social work base of the greater part of its history. For Jenny Roberts, the shift away from the social work ethos was one of the major changes 'which really stand out' during her probation experience. Interestingly, the strongest case for an enduring emphasis upon social work skills and values was made by the interviewee most closely identified with employer interests, Rodney Carroll, who suggested that

> one of the important features in probation has always been the relationship between the member of staff and the individual offender. To let the individual feel that there is someone there whom they could turn to and to whom, as an individual they were accountable, rather

than an organization . . . It is through the skill developed in that relationship that you actually protect the public. That must continue . . . I still think that you can do that while still at the same time care for them, and care about them as human beings. If we lose that we will become simply mechanistic controllers and that is never what the Probation Service has been about, and I hope it never will be. There is a place for social work values and ethics [in a service which is delivered] in the least regimented way possible because I don't think a regimented probation service would work. Probation officers have to be walking the streets of their communities and working on those streets, and that is where they need to be.

Cordell Pillay developed something of the same argument. She suggested that the 'non-criminal agenda' was one which both supported individuals and met the needs of the wider community, in the contribution which addressing the 'social context' of probationers' lives provided to crime reduction.

Richard Green echoed some of the same views, while making it clear that, if a conflict were to arise between the interests of welfare and the protection of the public, then the remit of probation service lay unambiguously in favour of the latter:

The welfare of the offender and the protection of the public can go together. By working on the rehabilitation of the offender, looking at why the offender is offending and what can be done to prevent reoffending, you are reducing the risk to the public and protecting the public. But it has been made very clear that if there is a conflict between those two then the protection of the public comes first. That is quite a clear change in what the probation service is about.

This sense of a service moving away from welfare and towards a correctional model was the dominant thread which ran through the views of all respondents.

Staff

Views of main-grade staff in probation provided one of the points around which views of respondents differed most sharply. For some, such as Richard Green – as set out below – staff represent the greatest asset of the service. Helen Schofield described that asset as residing in 'a kind of cultural cohesion about . . . wanting to help stop people getting into trouble' – a basic commitment to the essential purpose of the organization which binds people together. In a period of rapid change, others such as Cordel Pillay complained that 'the practitioners have not been prepared for change. By that I mean they've not been give the proper training . . . they've not been consulted. They've not been given the skills needed for change.' At a managerial level, Andrew Underdown emphasized the responsibility of the service to make sure that all staff experienced new ways of working towards that shared and enduring end as 'truly supportive rather than overbearing or inappropriate and misunderstood'.

For others, the situation appeared to be very different with staff, rather than being an asset, emerging as a source of resistance to necessary change. Sue Winfield went some of the way towards this view in a suggestion that resistance to change continued more at a covert than overt level amongst staff. Speaking of the shift from an autonomous to a managed service she suggested: 'You will always get a few ostriches, [but] intellectually, conceptually, the majority have got hold of it. I think there are still problems in how that's translated into practice because they may believe one thing and still do the old thing.' Linda Jones went further. In her view, the contemporary service had been created through a paradigm shift in its purpose and means of operation. In Leicestershire, she reported, a new rehabilitation programme had resulted in 'getting rid of most of our other programmes'. In encompassing such a 'very difficult cultural shift', not all staff were willing or able to 'take the huge jump'.

> There's been a real shift to accepting that the service's primary function is in relation to public protection and the assessment and management of risk. I don't think that has sufficiently established itself throughout the whole of the service yet, and I think many probation officers belong to a prior era in terms of welfare law.

For Linda Jones, the management of the service needed to take more assertive action, in order to overcome the residue of worker autonomy and to reinforce central control:

> I personally don't really understand why we've never grappled with the issue about national standards enforcement, and how the culture of the

service actually militates against that, and sees it as a choice . . . it can't be left up to individuals, especially the individual probation officer . . . I think we've got to get into a different culture.

Training

The interviews reported in this chapter were conducted at a time when previous training arrangements for probation officers had come to an end and when new courses were in the early stages of introduction. One of the consequences of these changes for service managers lay in a new difficulty in appointing trained workers. As Richard Green noted, 'We have posts we can't fill because we can't recruit qualified staff.' Asked to consider the scope for taking on new duties in PTS, Sue Winfield also suggested that for some services it wouldn't just be about money – 'They can't even get the staff at the moment.' For Jenny Roberts, the problem seemed even more acute:

There is a worrying lack of probation officers. I hope I'm wrong but there is a very strong conviction around that we are going to have to manage for a couple of years without being able to fill probation officer vacancies, and this could be catastrophic, because the credibility, the morale, all the things essential to the service could be missing.

The retention of training within higher education institutions was welcomed by all those who commented upon it. As Rodney Carroll suggested:

I've always been an advocate of having a degree programme of training for social workers and probation officers because it makes a statement about the particular value of such an employee. In the courts, where probation officers operate, they are surrounded by other highly qualified professionals and need to be seen as equally highly qualified.

Yet the same respondent pointed to the need to ensure continuity between old and new training arrangements. Too great an emphasis upon the contrast between new ways as 'good', and old ways as 'bad' would, he argued, 'imply to existing staff that their qualification was of little or no value. No employer worth their salt could say that and I dislike intensely any approach which writes away and denies the skill base of existing probation staff.' Making the same point – 'I deplore very very strongly any diversion from training in terms of the impact on the morale of the service' – Jenny Roberts nonetheless went on to suggest that the new training arrangements could offer a chance to concentrate upon core probation skills and to create a continuum of training from pre-qualifying to post-qualifying levels.

Local control?

A theme which preoccupied a number of interviewees concerned the ownership of the Probation Service, in the sense of its management either at local level or as a direct arm of central government. Unsurprisingly, perhaps, as a voice identified with the then current system of local probation committees, Rodney Carroll presented the case for maintaining the local dimension of the service and the representation of local interests in the delivery of its work: 'Crime is a local phenomenon which needs a response to that crime locally.' The fact that, however directly policy might be formulated at a national level, its implementation can only occur on a local basis argued, he suggested, for a powerful local representation in the oversight of that implementation. These views found support elsewhere. Richard Green put it simply: 'My vision is not for a national probation service.' Linda Jones, by contrast, favoured the opposite route:

> I do personally hope it will become a national service. We've resisted it for a long time during my career as chief probation officer, but I'd come already before I came to the prison service to that view . . . The Probation Service has never been able to compete in the same way for resources unless they were actually part of the centre . . . I also think there's a huge duplication in the Probation Service which leads to inconsistencies, unnecessary inconsistencies. I do think that it's worth having a national service.

As to the local probation committee,

> I've thought for a long time they should go. I think they're anachronistic and have done for a long time. There are some super people on them, a huge commitment, huge drive, tremendously supportive and excellent, but I think you could actually use that expertise in local communities without having employers and policy makers for individual committees.

Helen Schofield, while agreeing that local committees were not genuinely accountable, was in favour of a different solution:

> I wouldn't leave them out. I think you would want to move towards a much more locally elected structure [but] including key organizations you would want to see represented there – social services, voluntary organizations, as well as what's begun to open up around constructive community partnerships.

Core characteristics

Finally, in this section, and in an attempt to identify their most fundamental positions, interviewees were asked a series of questions about those core characteristics which, in their view, represented the essence of the Probation Service. Two distinctive schools of thought emerged, one which placed emphasis upon the more traditional, public service ethos of probation, while the second provided a more instrumental, managerialist perspective.

Asked to identify the unique contribution of the probation service, which was not to be found in any of the work of any other criminal justice organization, Rodney Carroll chose to emphasize the role of humanitarian broker which he saw in the work of the service:

> That blend of public protection and the ability to handle problems which sit in that arena while, at the same time being able to engage with all the issues which arise in relation to human beings – human development, psychology and generally caring about people. Probation, it seems to me, has brought those two different kinds of frictions together and enabled people to operate through that process in order to maintain offenders in the community.

Sue Winfield, dealing with the same issues, suggested that the service's most important distinguishing characteristic lay in 'our ability to work with offenders and motivate them to change'. For Jenny Roberts, the core lay in the public service ethos of probation:

> I'm not very anti-privatized concerns, but the point that I'm making is that the people who run them are not motivated to try to improve society, they're motivated to make money . . . there are values which probation officers have which do make a difference. You don't, when running a probation service, have to have concerns about abuse.

Identifying an allied characteristic within the same field, Helen Schofield suggested that, from her new perspective, the Probation Service stood out as an 'organization that has got a way of doing things, systems and procedures that sometimes get in the way, but by and large are facilitating and enabling'. That 'way of doing things' represented a shared understanding of purpose within the service which, in her view, provided 'a strength, in that it doesn't abandon things quickly'.

Amongst those who suggested a more instrumental rationale for the probation service, Graham Smith specifically rejected any 'words about humanitarianism, because that is not what the community pay the probation service to do'. Indeed, for Smith, the whole notion of a 'unique contribution' was questionable: 'Of course another organization could do the work of the Probation Service. It is not inevitable that a Probation Service is required to do the job it does.' Such 'unique features' as he could identify within present arrangements were clustered around 'measures of expediency' – the reduction of offending, the protection of the public and a set of outcomes that achieved these aims more successfully than custody. Framing essentially the same notions more positively, he suggested:

> The unique feature of a Probation Service is that it offers a community opportunities of dealing with offending and that its key unique features are its predictive abilities, in terms of predicting crime. That requires skill, training and competencies that are specific and important. It creates a fugitive skill, and by fugitive I mean a skill which you would lose if you did not practise it . . . There is a body of knowledge and information which exists out there which suggests what works and which holds together a respectable body of people who become probation officers.

Having explored the understanding which interviews provided of the most significant traits and trends in the contemporary state of probation, the remainder of this chapter now moves to consider the future prospects for the service, as viewed by interview respondents and, in particular, to their understanding of the place which pre-trial services might hold in that future.

Probation futures

The single most consistent theme in looking to the future for probation was to be detected in the emphasis which almost all respondents placed upon the development of the 'what works' movement. 'I am', said Rodney Carroll, 'a strong advocate of the 'what works' programme . . . There are certainly some styles and programmes which work better than others and we need to know much about the whole question of practice effectiveness and how that can be measured and achieved.' While there was some hesitation at what Jenny Roberts called 'magic bullet' solutions, the importance of this aspect of future practice was discussed in every single interview. For some, 'what works' was primarily a means of demonstrating to political masters that the service was worth its annual investment. For others, 'what works' went beyond the pragmatic and offered a means of retaining a distinctive Probation Service approach in a relatively hostile climate. Jenny Roberts put it this way:

> Intervention must be based on what is known about what works and not solely on theories of punishment or justice . . . I don't think that we should actually be here to deliver a punishment. I think we should be here to be the one group of people that really works with offenders at every stage.

Very few voices were raised in questioning the effectiveness agenda. One was to be found in Richard Green, who suggested that 'my worry is that I'm not convinced that research can demonstrate that probation service activity is effective. It is not the same as scientific research, this is social scientific research and it is much harder to draw conclusions about human behaviour.' Cordell Pillay put it differently: 'I think there seems to be so much pinned on effectiveness and what works that it's almost as if it's a panacea for everthing . . . a nuclear strategy . . . almost like putting all your eggs in one box.'

A second theme which united a series of contributors lay in what Cordell Pillay called the need 'for probation to recognize what it's good at'. For Rodney Carroll, the key task which lay ahead of the Probation Service was to place its confidence in the contribution which it makes through professional practice and to let that confidence – 'rather than simply ways which allow politicians and managers to decide about resource allocation' – shape its future. Jenny Roberts offered something of the same contrast, lamenting that 'we have been dragged off course recently', and asserting the importance of recapturing the social, as well as the criminal justice dimensions in a future direction for probation – 'the system is out of balance. We need to be part of solutions to social problems as well as crime.'

For Graham Smith, the essential future of probation lay in confirming its centrality to other players in the criminal justice system: 'The Probation Service offers a cradle-to-grave service within the criminal justice system. It is the only part of the system which is required to have links with all the other players, statutory and voluntary. It is the only one which has direct relationships with all the others at the same time.' In the further development of these links lay the future.

It was left to Helen Schofield to articulate a vision which placed probation in a wider community justice context. Starting from the premise that 'it is often people from the Probation Service who have the widest view about why crime occurs', she wished to draw probation into sharing its knowledge and expertise more by 'living much more actively within the community'. That would be a 'real role to play' in a future criminal justice agenda.

Pre-trial services and the future of probation

While all the interviewees included in this chapter possessed an in-depth knowledge of the Probation Service, they brought a wider range of direct experience of pre-trial services. Rodney Carroll reported a 'rather skimpy' involvement. Graham Smith, by contrast, had occupied a 'pivotal role' as the chief probation officer who chaired the group that set up bail information and bail support services and involvement in public interest case assessment work. Whatever the state of personal involvement, however, all respondents in this survey shared a considerable enthusiasm for the future development of pre-trial services. 'For me' said Jenny Roberts,

> pre-trial services are the absolute key to enable us and other scarce resources to be concentrated where they are really important . . . while continuing, at a time of specializing and working with very persistent and dangerous offenders, to have a stake in that vast sector of working with offenders which is about low levels of risk.

It is a development, said Helen Schofield, which was 'hugely needed'.

The 'logical nonsense' which Rodney Carroll identified in a system which holds so many people on remand who will not eventually receive a custodial sentence ran as a unifying theme in the enthusiastic support for pre-trial services which was apparent in all the interviews reported here. For Graham Smith, the growth in the remand population would provide the 'strongest and irresistible drive' behind future expansion of PTS in Britain. The fundamentally different nature of a diversionary approach was emphasized, as well, by Richard Green, who suggested that:

> I personally don't believe that prosecution, taking someone through the court system, is the only way to deal with offending behaviour. It's something that's not in vogue these days . . . because at the moment there does seem to be a culture whereby prosecution through the courts is the only answer to offending behaviour.

Noting the 1998 Crime and Disorder Act provision in youth justice, he concluded: 'I would like to see something developed along those lines for adults. I don't think we've explored the potential of that enough yet.'

Given his history of involvement, it is not, perhaps surprising that one of the most informed accounts of the rationale for a revival of pre-trial services within probation came from the chief inspector of probation, Graham Smith. His summary of the position is worth recording in some detail:

> Pre-trial services have always struck me as being essential because they get to the situation at an early stage, especially with the remand population, which is the fastest-growing within the prison system. When you are remanded you do not get the same sort of services you get when you are on bail. It is a dangerous period for the individual . . . so the Probation Service has a duty to provide information, and, in my eyes, a duty to help people who are in a particular crisis in their lives and so influence their offending career . . . Pre-trial services seem to me to be founded on something so fundamentally obvious that they should prosper and be a significant part of the remit of the Probation Service.

The views expressed by Graham Smith were to be common ground amongst almost all respondents. Additional points to emerge included an emphasis upon the particular opportunities which the Probation Service has at its disposal in providing pre-trial services. For one thing, as Sue Winfield emphasized, ' we've carried the flag and kept bail information alive' during a difficult period when support for that area of work had ebbed away nationally. Secondly, at the point of delivery, the same respondent suggested that 'one of the things that we have to remember is that it has been shown to us that 70 per cent of people who come into the court setting are already known to us'. Others pointed to the positive harm which can occur during a period of imprisonment, not simply in relation to the severing of ties with the outside world, but also in relation to the level of crime committed within prisons. Richard Green was not alone in pointing to the impact which bail experience can have upon sentencing outcome: 'A good period of bail support will add to the likelihood of the court's willingness to allow the Probation Service to work with that person in the community, when it comes to the point of sentence.'

In expressing support for pre-trial services it seems likely that the articulation of respondents' views was influenced by the apparently positive change in the climate of government opinion towards this aspect of Probation Service activity. At the 'Bail or Jail?' conference, Lord Mostyn made some of this enthusiasm clear: 'What I would like to emphasize most of all today is the importance that the government places on the development of efficient and effective bail information schemes.' Nor was bail information the only aspect of PTS to receive support: 'The government strongly believes that effective bail support schemes can also make an important contribution to ensuring that defendants awaiting trial or sentence successfully complete their period of bail.' A new key performance indicator was to be developed which would be backed up by new money to enable local services to renew work in the bail information area. The minister's speech ended with a call which reflects the purpose of this book, 'Some very good things are happening around the country. The challenge now is to make that best practice universal throughout England and Wales.'

Given the universal enthusiasm for pre-trial services, it was important to explore respondents' explanations for the lack of progress which had been achieved in providing such services from the mid-1990s onwards. Three sets of explanation emerged – the generally hostile attack upon probation during this period, as discussed above, together with financial and ethical considerations which are explored in more detail below. Only Cordell Pillay drew attention to the lack of value which had been attached to pre-trial work within the service, arguing that for 'the practitioner grade it is often a step back . . . it doesn't seem to be an integral part of the service'.

Money again

Across many of the interviews conducted for this chapter a theme emerged which identified the perverse disincentives which can result when the expenditure costs of change fall on one element within a whole system, while the cost benefits accrue to another. Pre-trial services reduce expenditure across the criminal justice system as a whole. The savings, however, primarily fall to the prison system, in terms of a reduced remand population. For the Probation Service, by contrast, pre-trial services represent more work and more expenditure, without – in financial terms – any compensating savings elsewhere. The resolution of this dilemma, according to Graham Smith, lay in persuading the Home Office that

> they get a return for their money further up the line in criminal justice, and that is not easy to prove . . . but I think that, in principle, pre-trial services *could* save money. That is why I am confident that we will see an expansion, a renewing of interest in the work.

Ethical issues and PTS

For the great majority of respondents here, the ethical dilemmas which have been sharply debated in relation to the intervention in the lives of individuals who have been charged, but not found guilty of any offence, were fairly easily resolvable. For the majority, it was, as Rodney Carroll expressed it, 'about balances to be struck between the benefits which the individual might derive and the impact upon their prospects within the system'. For others, such as Graham Smith,

> the civil and human rights issue is very easily resolved. You invite persons themselves to decide if they want you to work with them at that stage. And if they say no, that's what you accept. What I find

intolerable is the notion that you would make that decision for them
. . . that is a very arrogant, precious view to take of another person's
civil rights.

The strength of feeling which emphasizes the advantages of
intervention at the pre-trial stage can be found in Richard Green's
reminder that:

> If you've ever sat in an overnight arrests court, as I have on many
> occasions, and you have thirty or forty people who have been produced
> by the police for an offence and who have been held in custody
> overnight, you see the crisis, you see the family members in the public
> gallery, and it is an opportunity to influence people to intervene in their
> lives in a way that may change their behaviour in the future. If you leave
> that until the point of sentence, which could be several months after the
> alleged offence was committed, you may have missed the opportunity,
> the crisis may have passed. I do think that it is a legitimate thing to do
> within the scope of pre-trial services.

Nevertheless, some ethical issues did emerge in discussion. Sue
Winfield, one of the closest supporters of pre-trial services, argued
nevertheless that the labelling potential of intervention at the pre-
trial stage could make the case for the delivery of such services by
an organization other than probation. Helen Schofield suggested
that, if PTS were to be delivered by probation, then a clear
separation of role and functions would need to be maintained
between work with those who are unconvicted and those who are
being supervised as a result of an admission or finding of guilt. She
also drew attention to the way in which such considerations
'impact particularly on women and black people. Wherever there is
a lack of confidence then you have to be more careful about pre-
trial services.'

Conclusion

This chapter began by tracing some of the competing and
conflictual threads which have run through the recent history of the
Probation Service in England and Wales, suggesting that any single
point of view would be bound to represent a partial and relatively

perilous attempt to pick a path through these complexities. Against that background, it is hardly surprising that differences of emphasis emerge between the different views reported here. Against a general background, in which all are agreed about the pace of change and the shift from a welfare to a public protection focus in service work, respondents essentially ally themselves with one of two schools of thought. For some, the changes in the service are represented as retaining certain essential continuities with the past – the reapplication of principles of public service, active concern for those who offend, as well as those who are offended against, and a positive belief in the delivery of services through informed, critically aware practitioners. For others, service changes represent a more fundamental, and fruitful, break with the past. Here the future for probation lies in a hard-edged demonstration of its usefulness to the paying public, a usefulness which, in this view, might better be achieved through a more disciplined workforce, charged with the implementation of empirically informed practices which allow for little room for manoeuvre in their application upon – rather than with – individuals who break the law.

Given this diversity, the unanimity with which respondents expressed their support for pre-trial services is all the more striking. Whatever vision an individual held for the future of probation, the need for revived pre-trial initiatives was universally affirmed. Of course, hesitations remain – over financial arrangements, over civil liberty questions, over the involvement of probation itself in pre-trial services – but the principle of early, positive intervention was shared by all. Here, respondents seemed convinced, a means might be found by which individuals could be assisted and their greater rights – to maintain a home and to prepare a defence, for example – could be protected and promoted. Here, too, was a means by which the Probation Service could keep in touch with that vast bulk of the population appearing before the courts who do not represent a serious risk to their fellow citizens, but who are, far more, only embodiments of the ordinary frailties and misfortunes of those same citizens, writ larger. Finally, here was a means of assisting the whole system where that system found itself under greatest strain – in the escalating expenditure of money upon an ever-increasing remand population in prison. A policy development which holds out promise across such a range of desirable outcomes is rare in any area of government, but perhaps especially so in criminal justice. The need to do it well, and in a way which delivers its potential benefits, runs as a further theme in the views of the respondents reported here. It is, of course, the purpose of the research with which this whole book is engaged.

6. Conclusion

This book has considered the future of the Probation Service in England and Wales. While there has been no shortage of debate and speculation about that future, the account offered here differs in one crucial respect. It concentrates upon a neglected theme in contemporary practice and policy-making – but one which, it is argued, deserves to occupy a far more central position in the unfolding pattern of criminal justice. The arguments in support of effective remand management throughout the Probation Service hierarchy are many and range from the expedient through the practical to the ethical.

The evidence and views presented in this book argue strongly that pre-trial services can and do offer an effective, safe and humane solution. They argue that, as with other areas of criminal justice, there is a place for a community alternative to custody if it is managed with the skills and experience of the Probation Service. This book is the fruit of original research into the scope for and effectiveness of these pre-trial services. The clear aim has been to identify and investigate systems and services that could provide an alternative to a restrictive, often destructive and always costly remand in custody, whilst establishing that the alternative is equally able to protect and serve the best interests of public and defendant alike.

In looking at the role and potential role for the probation service in providing a service pre-trial this book is necessarily addressing itself to a wider audience. As each chapter makes clear in different ways, the work of the Probation Service must overlap and connect with the work of others to be effective, and decisions about remand management lie not only with practitioners and managers within the Probation Service but with policy-makers across the Home Office and with managers in prisons, courts, Crown Prosecution Service and police. This is not just in terms of shared purpose, but in agreements on communication, objectives and funding, particularly where one service gains from the effort of another. This is what we have called a proactive remand management strategy in which the needs of the courts to manage bail effectively in a safe and just way are met by the combined working of the agencies that serve them, within an inclusive legislative and policy framework.

This study has identified many gaps in a criminal justice system that lacks a proactive remand management strategy. These gaps relate in particular to the Bail Act and its application, to incomplete and badly maintained information systems, to the reliable provision of services and knowledge of them, to inter-agency co-operation, and to a lack of good independent research to identify what works in the remand system. In interview, magistrates have said that without suitable and effective alternatives to a remand in custody, or good evidence on which to base a decision, their options on bail are severely limited. The result has been in many cases the costly and arguably unnecessary imposition of custody for many whose risk to the public has not been clearly established and who subsequently receive a non-custodial sentence for their offence. As argued in chapter 1, this is 'institutionalized ambivalence' that has resulted often in the incarceration of the socially inadequate rather than the dangerous or serious offender. This study has therefore looked at the bail process, the scope for intervention at the pre-trial stage, and the range of existing services to identify how they might be applied justly and effectively in the courts each day. The study has looked in particular at the scope for developing a national pre-trial service using the skills and resources of the Probation Service.

Firstly, the findings from this study have arisen from a number of original pieces of research. Examination of the evidence and data has been critical and cautious, and the lessons from the evidence are offered with due acknowledgement of their limitations. Secondly, there has also been a strong commitment to examining the evidence with other pressing public agendas in mind. Would pre-trial services work? Would they constitute good value for money and are they likely to form an effective part of the wider criminal justice system (including management of risk, crime reduction, inter-agency partnership and social inclusion)?

In examining these questions, strong support has emerged for the principles and practice of pre-trial services. This endorsement was evident in four ways.

Firstly, the available evidence demonstrates that pre-trial services (including bail information, bail support and work in hostels with bailees) currently offer a cheaper and effective alternative to a remand in custody for a substantial number of defendants.

Secondly, the service provided is an effective alternative to custody which also addresses issues of public risk, has a good record of returns to court, and employs a range of community support programmes in the spirit of joined-up policy and inter-agency partnership.

Thirdly, pre-trial services have the confidence and support of magistrates, prosecutors, managers and policy-makers, who almost universally welcomed and valued its contribution to the criminal justice system.

Lastly, there is scope for expanding the present pre-trial services provision and initiating a proactive remand management strategy. This is based both on the lessons learnt from the schemes researched and from the examination of the current nature of remand management. In addition the resource implications for the Probation Service in developing a pre-trial service dimension to its current work, and its benefits, have been investigated and the development of a national pre-trial service found on current evidence to be cost-effective.

Summary of main findings

This project began by setting out four objectives:

(a) to make some estimate of the present scale of pre-trial services in England and Wales,
(b) to investigate the nature and quality of existing services in this field,
(c) to estimate the potential impact of a revived pre-trial capacity upon the current decisions made at the remand stage, and
(d) to estimate the level of support within the service for such an initiative.

It would be logical, therefore to revisit those objectives in summing up the findings of the book as a whole. Each of these points has been addressed fully, however, in the preceding chapters, and it is perhaps unnecessary to rehearse those points again for the reader under the same headings. What might be more productive here is to return to the purpose of this project and to ask what these findings can now contribute to the pre-trial debate. How nearer are we to asserting that pre-trial services can and should play a major role in our criminal justice system? The answer to that question lies in answering three more: What is the evidence that pre-trial services work? What is already in place to support a national pre-trial service, and what is missing? What needs to be done if we are to develop a national pre-trial service?

What is the evidence that pre-trial services work?

To work, pre-trial services need to function like other parts of the Probation Service. They need the support and confidence of policy-makers, practitioners and sentencers. They need a body of research evidence to show that they are able to meet their own stated objectives as part of the community justice system, and they need to fit in with wider public agendas such as risk management, social inclusion and value for money. This book has shown that pre-trial work meets all three criteria.

General support

Support for pre-trial work is, as has been said many times, very strong and almost universal across the criminal justice world. Chapter 3 presents a good many views of magistrates, prosecutors, practitioners, managers and clients who all praised the worth of effective bail information and bail support schemes in particular. For example, within the court system one magistrate said, 'We need to make difficult decisions very quickly and anything that can be done to help us in that is very welcome.' A prosecutor put it this way: 'In court there is insufficient time for us to find good information. The bail information officer is seen as an independent source of helpful information.'

In chapter 5 the views of influential managers and policy-makers are recorded and again found to be universally in favour of pre-trial work. Graham Smith, chief inspector of probation, for example, said:

Pre-trial services have always struck me as being essential because they get to the situation at an early stage, especially with the remand population, which is the fastest-growing within the prison system . . .

Pre-trial services seem to me to be founded on something so fundamentally obvious that they should prosper and be a significant part of the remit of the Probation Service.

From the employers' side, the 'logical nonsense', which Rodney Carroll identified in a system which holds so many people on remand who will not eventually receive a custodial sentence, ran as a unifying theme in the enthusiastic support for pre-trial services, which was apparent in all the interviews reported in chapter 5. For Graham Smith, the growth in the remand population would provide the 'strongest and most irresistible drive' behind future expansion of pre-trial services in Britain.

Evidence

Bail information

With such strong support it is surprising that there is so little remand-orientated practice within the Probation Service. In this regard, the service provided is inconsistent and of variable quality. However, in the few probation areas that properly support pre-trial services, the evidence of its success is striking. Clearly the data presented in this book must therefore rely on a small sample. In chapters 2 and 3 the available evidence on pre-trial interventions was investigated, and within the limitations of the small-scale studies available it provided a clear endorsement. For example a total of 83 per cent of defendants concluded their time on the WMPS bail support programme without reoffending (WMPS 1997). This finding was echoed by research in several other probation areas and in the three areas investigated in detail in chapter 3. Bail information was found to provide information which was effective in diverting defendants towards bail support or other community disposals, and bail support itself was demonstrably ensuring compliance with bail conditions. This compliance was substantially greater than the norm identified in earlier studies of bailees by Raine and Willson (1994) (see chapter 4).

Wider public agendas

Similarly the available evidence as presented in chapters 1 and 2 supports the assertion that bail support and bail information initiatives in particular are able to meet the requirements of risk management. The public is demonstrably protected if bail packages are well targeted, if the information on which bail decisions are made is accurate and full, and if the strategies for managing defendants on bail are effective. The evidence presents a picture of greater likelihood of compliance with bail if bail information and bail support services are applied, and this is despite the many flaws identified within the current system. A well-managed, well-resourced and integrated system, as we shall discuss later, could justifiably be expected to do even better.

The best-value agenda is also addressed in this study. In chapters 1 and 4 a number of scenarios are rehearsed in which the cost-effectiveness of projected national pre-trial services is compared with the current cost of remands in custody.

Pritchard (in Pritchard and Cox 1996) did a cost-benefit analysis of the Dorset Schemes starting from the hypothesis that each crime costs the taxpayer £2,700. He estimated that the successful diversion of 300 heroin-dependent people in east Dorset would provide savings for the criminal justice system amounting to £2,737,500. Conversely, he argued, we could abandon any notion of rehabilitation and send them all to prison, which in the case of east Dorset would cost the taxpayer £62,188,000. This was apart from prison's poorer rate of recidivism compared with probation.

On a national scale chapter 5 addresses the savings more comprehensively. Remand prisoners, of course, do not normally spend more than a few weeks in custody. Thus the average daily population of remand prisoners is about 12,000 (of whom two-thirds are unsentenced) (White and Woodbridge 1998). A fully effective national pro-active bail management strategy might, therefore, be expected to reduce the average daily prison population by about 6,000.

Based on Home Office estimates (Harries 1999) the average cost of a remand prisoner is £5,000. Working with this figure, an estimate of the total cost of the remand population is £300,000,000. A comprehensive and effective proactive bail management strategy might, therefore, be expected to save £150 million per year – at current rates and costs. In chapter 4 there is also an exploration of new evidence that a high proportion of defendants who are remanded in custody are subsequently found to be not guilty, or more commonly that the case against them is dismissed or a non-custodial sentence given. There is also strong evidence to support the effectiveness of community disposals that at worst are no less able to prevent future offending than custody. Chapter 2 examines a number of research studies that support the view that community rehabilitation has a higher success rate than custodial alternatives. In chapter 3 are examinations of successful bail support schemes, one of which, for example, demonstrated a 68 per cent completion rate out of 140 young offenders on bail support schemes, of whom only 5 per cent re-offended whilst on bail. Those defendants themselves reported the success of the scheme in their eyes, offering a genuine opportunity to repair the damage caused to their lives and those of others by their offending.

Logically it follows, too, that there is as much a place for probation supervision in the community at the pre-trial stage as there is post-sentence and post-custody. The skills and expertise of the probation service in delivering that service are as likely to succeed with well-selected defendants as with convicted criminals – they are the same people! The research has also described ways in which pre-trial work has developed as a model of inter-agency co-operation. Two schemes worked closely with the police, and six were engaged in partnership with voluntary-sector partners or social services.

This is a summary of the positive evidence, which emerged in support of pre-trial services. What then was the extent of the systems already existing?

What is already in place to support a national pre-trial service, and what is missing?

The reply to this question lies in three factors. Support for the idea of pre-trial work, the services and expertise at hand to be learned from and used, and the current legislative and policy framework.

Support for the idea of pre-trial work

Amongst the influential list of probation managers interviewed in chapter 5 there is firm support for a pre-trial service. Given the diversity of other views, the unanimity with which respondents expressed their support for pre-trial services is all the more striking. Whatever vision an individual held for the future of probation, the need for revived pre-trial initiatives was universally affirmed. Of course, hesitations remain – over financial arrangements, over civil liberty questions, over the involvement of probation itself in pre-trial services – but the principle of early, positive intervention was shared by all.

This support is surprising in its unanimity, but needs to be taken cautiously in one regard – it has not as yet been translated into any tangible advance in developing a pre-trial service on what existed four or five years before the hypothecated funding was withdrawn.

Within the services itself there was strong support from those who had any direct connection with pre-trial work. This included managers and senior managers, probation officers and assistants. This work was, however, isolated and under threat from those who had no direct contact with it. In all three of the areas studied, themselves selected because of their previous commitment to pre-trial work, the service had been reduced substantially over the past three years. Since the research project began one of the areas has retrenched further, with the current chief probation officer no longer committing core funding to pre-trial work in future.

In the wider criminal justice system, amongst those sentencers, clerks and prosecutors interviewed in chapter 3 there was also strong support for pre-trial work where they were aware of it. Again, though, ignorance of the work and its processes undermined that support. A few were not aware of it at all, and amongst those who were, none knew, for example, of the special conditions attached to bail support and bail hostels that would ensure compliance and assist rehabilitation. As with the policy formers, support in principle outweighed support in action. In particular, there was a strong belief amongst hostel staff that bail hostels, already available nationally with experienced staff and access to community resources, are consistently undervalued and underused. Bail support programmes of the kind investigated in chapter 3 could well be developed around existing hostel provision with their emphasis on support, rehabilitation, risk management and service to the courts and public.

Chapter 3 examines a good body of selected services which have provided a strong base for pre-trial work and have provided good models from which to draw evidence, skills and ideas which could sustain a move to providing similar schemes nationally.

The services and expertise at hand to be learned from and used

The pre-trial services examined critically in chapter 3 offered a number of models of good practice that might be profitably developed or copied nationally. The integrated model operating a bail support and bail information service within one probation service unit, with a full-time managing SPO and PO to co-ordinate and evaluate the work, and direct access to one ACPO, was the most demonstrably successful. It had developed expertise and practice that sustained a high success rate, and overcame many of the pitfalls of the pre-trial services 'added on' to existing services. These, operating bail information within the court service and bail support through partnership money, reported marginalization of the work and difficulties in particular in maintaining consistent flows of information between elements of the service.

The evidence collected for chapter 3 also identified the need to develop better communication networks within the probation service and across the criminal justice system. Good models of bail information and support were undermined by a lack of good information and a lack of a culture of co-operation across agencies both in keeping informed about defendants and in working together to support and rehabilitate them. There were also excellent aspects of the work, in particular the return to court service operated by bail support schemes and the rehabilitative programmes operated in hostels, which were underused because others within the criminal justice system were not aware of them.

Nevertheless, partnership bail support projects had at least sustained a strong social work ethos in delivering demonstrably successful bail support programmes, with the added benefit of enhanced inter-agency co-operation. The pitfalls were largely attributable to poor and uncertain resourcing, which must be addressed in a nationally endorsed scheme. The competition for funding from core work was a drain on the support and investment that these projects needed in order to develop, and indifference from other probation teams was undermining their success.

Key lessons, however, were clear. Bail information work was making an impact on sentencing through careful collection of verified information. Bail support was working successfully with bailees and reducing both reoffending and absconding rates by offering a support service similar to pre-CJA probation supervision. Hostels were working successfully with high-risk bailees in addressing offending and social problems with a range of expertise and services. All of these services had begun to collect data to confirm their success, and to identify areas of skill and expertise.

What was missing was substantial, however. Firstly, the scarcity of projects. The first phase of this project has already identified the scarcity of bail support work and the patchy application of bail information work (Haines and Octigan 1999). This study has in addition reported in chapter 3 the reduction in size and funding of even the current bail support schemes. This is itself an indictment of the readiness of the Probation Service to rise to a new opportunity. As detailed in chapter 2, the few attempts within the Probation Service to rise to the challenge of the hypothecated funding in the early 1990s left very little to show for such a specific opportunity.

The end of hypothecated funding in 1995 was predicated upon the contention that support for pre-trial services would be absorbed within mainstream probation budgets. In fact, the withdrawal of dedicated monies coincided with severe cuts in core funding for the Probation Service as a whole. In the inevitable horse-trading between different demands which followed, pre-trial budgets were considerably reduced in most areas and, in some, disappeared altogether. At the same time, the number of people entering prison rose to record levels, without any parallel rise in funding. The demands of maintaining security soon overwhelmed the provision of bail information in prison settings, as chapter 2 recorded.

The marginalization of pre-trial work is explicable under these conditions. It indicates, though, that more will need to happen before pre-trial work can move from being just a good idea to a national reality. Before examining that, however, the legal and policy framework deserves some attention.

The legal and policy framework

Some of the political and financial conditions necessary to the success of an active remand management strategy are discussed above and in chapter 2. Also central to a successful strategy is support within the court system itself. The support of court officials and magistrates for pre-trial work has been noted, and the mechanism under the Bail Act for the use of bail information and bail support is clearly described in chapter 2. As noted in chapter 4, 'the process of sentencing relies heavily on the provision of information to the court', and this in itself is an open invitation for the development of a full national bail information system. The powers under the Bail Act to withhold bail are also clear, and the fear in particular of reoffending and absconding are addressed directly in the work of bail support programmes with bailees.

These are strengths. What is less favourable to the development of a successfully managed bail process is the way that these powers are applied.

Chapter 4 identified a clear weakness in the current bail scheme. Bail itself has been a neglected area of criminal justice, with confusion and overlap between different components within the system. An absence of coherence is characteristic of the whole business of bail, from policy to practice. No single agency has responsibility for the system. As a result, accountability suffers and the basic building-blocks of informed understanding are neglected.

Three issues stand out here: The Bail Act, which can be punitive in its application; the decision-making process itself, which can be incoherent; and thirdly, the lack of a universal and effective computerized information system to be used across the court and criminal justice system. All three will need addressing if bail is to be successfully managed.

What needs to be in place to make a pre-trial service work?

There is clearly no shortage of arguments in support of a national pre-trial service, or of evidence or models on which that service might draw. There also appears to be strong support for the idea amongst those who would be expected to initiate, support, manage, implement or use it. So why do we not have one, what might change that, and how?

Why do we not have one?

The problems of implementing a pre-trial service, once funded, within the Probation Service are more to do with models of good practice than policy. These are discussed in more detail above and below, and in chapter 3. This section is more concerned with the wider agenda and what has been referred to in chapter 4 as the development of an integrated remand management strategy. The obstacles to this are worth rehearsing. Many problems have been identified as obstacles to the development of a national pre-trial service in the chapters of this book; in particular a lack of funding for pre-trial work, poor co-operation between the criminal justice agencies, and poor application of the Bail Act within the courts. The previous period of hypothecated funding showed that, where there was also a will within a probation area, some good projects would be developed, but these mostly died when funding was withdrawn. The lack of permanent dedicated funding has therefore meant that supporters of pre-trial work have not been able to argue for support from within the service. When other areas of practice are able to argue a greater priority, and are themselves under threat, pre-trial work is not going to survive.

The lack of key performance indicators for pre-trial work has reinforced this inferior status. On key performance indicators, chief probation officers are accountable at least to inspectors and to the Home Office for the delivery of services in their area, and those elements such as bail support which have none remain poor relations when funding is considered.

A further obstacle lies in poor inter-agency co-operation, particularly between prison and probation services. Work undertaken with bailees in prison appears on neither service's priorities, and time taken to manage referral systems and optimize chances for bailees are frequently lost, as discussed in chapter 3. To ensure inter-agency co-operation also needs a government strategy, since just as departments within each service are competing for funds, so services are themselves competing for funding from the Home Office. Since this project was completed, a part of the problem has been addressed. Bail information was made a key performance indicator jointly with the Prison Service in January 2000, and training of bail information officers has followed. More research will be needed to assess the impact of this change, and to argue for bail support to follow suit.

Finally, magistrates' practice in implementing the Bail Act needs attention from the Lord Chancellor's Department. Inconsistencies in practice of the kind identified in chapter 4 are not acceptable in a criminal justice system, particularly when the stakes in terms of public safety, individual liberties, the reputation of the court and public expense are so high. This is again a matter needing training and guidance on a national scale and a review of the Bail Act and its procedures as discussed in chapter 4 above.

So, just as all roads lead to Rome, the bolder solutions to the problems of developing a national remand management strategy and service therefore lie with central policy-makers rather than with local managers and practitioners.

Chapter 4 concludes with some strong statements on bail management. It argues that the necessity of widening the scope of a remand management strategy into a bail management strategy is derived from the findings that the whole area of bail decision making is much neglected and redolent of poor practice. There is thus an overriding need for an agency to get to grips with bail, and to take responsibility for managing this aspect of criminal justice practice and for improving the quality of justice and practice in the area of bail.

At the present time, national and local policies and objectives for bail do not exist in any meaningful form since the information required to develop these policies is simply not available. The potential scope for remand services to have a significant impact on the bail process is dependent upon the routine production of good-quality, robust information backed up by effective services. The development of national and local policies for bail and the development of remand services is thus contingent upon the promotion of a proactive bail management strategy.

Back to the local services

In this way the argument may in some ways be seen to come full circle. If policy-makers are to adopt a national pre-trial service they need to be convinced that public money is being well spent by so doing. To prove that, practitioners and managers need to develop and assess reliably a robust and successful scheme which makes both strategic and economic sense. Only then can it be argued strongly that a good pre-trial service can address the problem of a growing remand population by offering safe and successful alternatives.

To a large extent this book attempts to bridge just that gap. The arguments in favour of pre-trial work have been summed up, and they make the case for adoption of these projects on a national scale. Having restated them in this Conclusion, the circle will be completed if the baton is passed back to the services themselves. Although the available evidence points to a success rate in bail information, hostels and support that compares well with rates for reoffending or absconding on bail or recidivism after custody, the evidence in chapter 3 also highlighted much that could be improved within the pre-trial provisions themselves. If these services could be improved they could logically be expected to perform better, and therefore offer an even more attractive alternative to the vastly expensive remands in custody. There is at the time of writing a good opportunity to lobby policy-makers whilst probation funding is less tight and support for pre-trial work is apparently strong. The force of that lobby will rest on the strength of the evidence in support of the work being undertaken. This, the evidence suggests, is a management task.

Beyond that, the Probation Service's contribution to pre-trial work is limited. The need, then, is for a policy framework in which the combined efforts of prison, court and police services are deployed with the Probation Service in managing the bail population proactively. This may need changes in the Bail Act to give courts the authority to manage risk within the community, clearer lines of responsibility for the agencies involved on information sharing and co-operation, and shared targets which reflect success in this new area of work. This, the evidence suggests, is a government task. What are needed primarily are better structures and funding to support and develop the existing pre-trial services. Just as with the Probation Service generally, better use of communication and evaluation systems, methods of developing good practice and disseminating it through training are needed to develop the full potential of pre-trial work. On a wider scale inter-agency co-operation, particularly between courts, probation, prison and social services would be an essential element of a good service. This would answer the needs of wider public agendas of joined-up policy, social inclusion and partnership. It is not therefore just a matter of funding and legislation but of good practice. With these, the argument for a fully developed national remand management strategy and pre-trial service would be irresistible. So, to return to the beginning: 'A vision for the future of remand services is one in which a fully articulated set of court-focused remand services, firmly located within the public protection and effectiveness agendas, can be mobilized to reduce, wherever possible, unnecessary and inappropriate remands in custody' (Haines and Octigan 1999).

Appendix

Research into models of good practice

This research was carried out over three separate week-long research visits to three separate probation areas. Recorded interviews were conducted across each area with the following.

Probation service staff
One CPO
Four ACPOs
Probation bail support staff (three SPOs, three probation officers)
Probation bail information staff (three SPOs, eleven bail information officers)
Two central bail referral officers

Partner agencies delivering bail support work
Three managers
Three bail support workers
One community psychiatric nurse
Three clients

Court staff
Two clerks
Four prosecutors
Six magistrates

Hostel staff
Four managers (SPO level)
Two hostel referral workers
Eight residents

Access was made to internal reports, records, evaluations, annual reviews and partnership contract documents across each area.

Questions asked of interviewees

What is your knowledge of pre-trial work?
What do you know of bail support work?
What do you know of bail information work?
How does your work contribute to the pre-trial process?
What responsibility do you have for pre-trial work of any kind?
Can you describe what you do and how it works?
What are your views on the success of pre-trial work in this area?
What strengths does it have?
What weaknesses does it have?
What do you think would improve this work?
Do you have any other comment to make?
Could I contact you for clarification later?

The hostel view

Hostels were responsible for accommodating a significant proportion of those on bail support programmes. They offered a variety of support and therapy programmes pre-trial for other defendants as well. The hostel managers interviewed had clear and strong views on the assessment process by which bailees were selected. In two of the three probation areas referrals to hostels were controlled by central bail referral officers, but in all cases the original referral and assessment of defendants was made by bail information officers at court.

Hostel managers were critical of what they saw as the shortfalls in this service, leading to missed or inappropriate referrals: 'Assessment at court is not up to it – we are not getting the right people. All those denied bail by police and the CPS should be interviewed. Assessment by bail information officers not enough.' 'The bail information officer sometimes says no to drugs being a problem but the resident turns out on arrival to be an addict.' And more specifically: 'Forty per cent of those bailed to the hostel do not arrive. Targeting is haphazard and needs more thought. The hostel is wrongly seen as a last-chance saloon – for up-tariff and severe cases only.' 'Risk criteria for bail are not properly applied. There is too short a time (at court) to take decisions which fully recognize the risk to other residents and to the public in the area, or to consider the risk of harm.'

The call was not for less bail information but for more emphasis on it. Hostel managers were asking for the role to be more professional with a thorough assessment process with more time and resources with which to do it. Like bail information, they also described hostels as a 'marginalized' and underappreciated arm of the probation service: 'We are perceived as having unqualified staff and poor practice. Hostels are not seen as part of the overall probation structure.'

They were by contrast enthusiastic about the programmes offered at hostels. Each hostel offered drug counselling, employment education and training programmes, group therapy, individual support work and structured leisure activities. As a means of improving the service the following suggestions were offered. One clearly identified area of need was in managing drug-using defendants: 'Defendants will hide their addiction to get bail. We need to set up guidelines for managing drug users in hostels. I would like to see drug users assessed by experts and clear conditions attached to bail for opiate users.' 'It would be effective if we could have a compulsory week in custody on de-tox before hostel admission.' And on mentally disordered offenders: 'A specialized hostel service could be more effective. Mentally disordered offenders in particular need a dedicated hostel. Their problems are camouflaged in mixed hostels and they need medication expertise.'

Overall hostels need clearer national standards (now developed). Communication with the wider service is poor, as is integration with field services.

The partners' view
The managers of the voluntary organizations delivering pre-trial services (bail support) raised a number of common issues. Most notable were the nature of their expertise, training and the difficulties of working with probation. On their distinct added value these comments were made: '[In recruitment] we look for people with the right philosophy who are good at communication, are committed and will go the extra mile.' 'The work tends to be small-scale and the service is finding a niche for itself. We have a more intensive focus for fifteen- to nineteen-year-olds, and are able to offer a twenty-four-hour response'. 'We don't have money; it's very much about what we give personally to the relationship.' 'We offer weekly counselling, help with benefits and family matters. It is very much a counselling, mentoring and advocacy approach but also with a supervisory and monitoring role. A lot of work is done with clients to avoid breach but we don't take on the breach so that doesn't cloud the relationship.'

Training and recruitment were difficult issues, chiefly because 'staff are on annual contracts which makes continuity difficult', 'because of scarce resources' and because 'we tend to attract the least qualified people because of salary and contract'. As one summarized it: 'There is a big turnover of staff. Staff are on twelve-month contracts, so training is difficult, but staff model roles for clients. There are ex-police, teachers and parents. A standardized induction follows recruitment. This includes our philosophy and role-play.' 'There are regular training and social events to provide cohesion. Training needs are linked to annual appraisals, and because of scarce resources are needs-led'.

One positive aspect to partnership was the role of probation in offering access to its in-house training free of charge as part of the contracts. On other issues, however, partners were mixed in their opinion of the Probation Service. Generally there seemed to be a lot of praise for individual probation managers who responded well to the partners and kept communication open, but on an institutional level there was strong criticism. 'The downside of partnership is the uncertainty and cuts. The statutory agency also tends to be the oppressive partner in the partnership. Their practice is oppressive. The voluntary sector is taken for granted.' And again more specifically: 'There is poor communication within probation and it often falls to our staff to explain practice and policy to probation staff because they are not aware of the contract or its implications. This is often met with a poor response and an attitude of indifference to the voluntary agency. There is no guarantee of co-operation or compliance.'

Finally, on the vexed issue of funding: 'The ACPO is supportive but it is still difficult to operate effectively on block funding. A unit price is not enabling – we are not able to show the quality of our work. If we put a ceiling on the numbers which we are working with it would break the spirit of the partnership, we would lose goodwill and efficiency and would be out of operation for part of the year.' 'With social services there is a five-year contract, which allows clarity and planning. With probation it is defined by unit cost, and the referral mechanism is rather crude and ill defined. The contract is open but the downside . . . is the uncertainty and cuts.'

The view from the bench

Magistrates interviewed in all three probation areas were consistent in their views of pre-trial services and the bail process on a number of points. Their praise for the usefulness of bail information was unanimous. 'We need to make difficult decisions very quickly and anything that can be done to help us in that is very welcome.' 'We rely on probation staff, and generally we see them as impartial, though with a tendency to err, shall we say, on the humane side.'

They also argued that the information should be full and given to them directly: 'I think it should be a service to the court. If the CPS want to object to bail they need to sustain those objections by reference to known facts – they need to base objections to bail on known information, and it should be available to all parties.'

The difficulty in getting hold of good information was not apparent, and the inconsistency of the type of information offered did not trouble magistrates. Some reported an awareness of the need for courts to wait for information to be verified but were supportive of this and had no perception of probation staff as anything other than helpful.

There was consensus too on the need for better systems of information. As one said:

> There is a lack of communication within the system. We need an impetus and motivation to bring sensible boundaries and common goals. If one service's improvement and basic costs benefit another, then that should be recognized in joint KPIs. We are beginning a worthwhile process of bringing management principles to bear on joint working.

On bail support there were mixed views only in their perception of what it was. Some had no experience of it and were generally unaware of what it meant for defendants: 'Our knowledge of bail support is thin. Our knowledge of hostels is better. I'm not aware of pre-trial services happening.' 'I see where it works but not where it doesn't. We aren't told that some information is not available.'

One of the very few dissenting voices on pre-trial work was a magistrate who questioned its fairness both to society and to the defendant: 'It's all very well if somebody wants help but we can't help, pre-trial. I'm not sure that there is a place for presupposing guilt.' On bail support: 'Linking education and employment with crime is not fair to those who do not commit crimes. A special service pre-trial is putting too many resources into criminals – it's bad enough helping the convicted as well as including the unconvicted too.'

This was, however, a lone voice amongst those interviewed. Most were positive about bail information, bail support and partnership, and saw their place in the wider criminal justice system: 'Partnership is a very welcome idea. The partner can do bail support and leave POs free to supervise offenders. It allows specialism on both sides.' On bail support 'It opens up the probation versus prison debate. It is difficult to find secure accommodation. Bail support could fill this gap.'

Prosecutors' view

One observation made by prosecutors was that in their opinion bail decisions were never too punitive and that the Bail Act was properly applied. The decisions were well informed and took good note of public safety. That the number of defendants remanded in custody was greater than that finally given a custodial sentence reflected the greater powers under the Bail Act. It was logical therefore to question the Bail Act and the powers which it gives for a remand in custody on grounds that would not even be considered at sentencing, such as having a stable address. As one put it:

> There are no more in custody than should be. Some courts are hard but not this one. We apply the Crown Court test to the magistrates' court. Bail is not given, particularly where past history indicates a failure. Also, where shoplifters commit offences on bail or are likely to, a remand in custody is justified.

They gave an insight into the issues on which they judged it reasonable to object to bail: 'In assessing bail a good address is high on the list, together with police objection. In domestic violence this is also an obvious need.'

On bail information their views were all positive:

> In court there is insufficient time for us to find good information. The bail information officer is seen as an independent source of helpful information. Credibility would be lost if the information were not true. The relationship with the bail information officer is good.

On the information itself they offered this advice: 'The most common and useful information is: residence, employment, current probation, family ties. Are they still taking the tablets? Are there children at the address?' Interestingly, it was observed that there is a better chance of bail for those defendants who enter the court from outside, not from the cells into the dock. These are seen by the bench as already from custody and are more likely to be sent back there.

On the issue of full information they were also clear: 'The CPS would prefer to have full information. The positive and negative is useful for court. In fact we would also like to see pre-sentence reports too. It benefits everybody in court if all information can be seen at the same time.' They also supported the idea of bail support and were familiar with the local schemes, showing an interest in what the probation service had to offer: 'There is a place for bail support – rehabilitation would be useful in the bail process. But there is a lack of information about hostels. We need to know what is going on in hostels and what is on offer.'

The bail information officers' view

The picture from the bail information officers interviewed was of trying to operate a system within many other different and sometimes contradictory systems. When talking about their own work, bail information officers spoke of trying to be systematic and consistent. In talking about the constraints, they all described the generally positive attitude from individuals within the court system but of pressures created by the unsympathetic systems in which they operated.

On the subject of developing their own expertise these comments were offered: 'We have developed our own system of targeting. We target those with no address, and then those with proximity of offence to home, partner etc.' 'If there is a hint of mental health we also target those defendants, and the vulnerable. We take account of offence seriousness, and the solicitor will also come with requests.' 'We would like to tap into the community projects available – particularly employment and drugs – but there is not enough time to do this.' 'I see bail information as a link from community to court at the bail stage – and between the court and the services available in the community. It is networking the court-to-community resources . . . More services in the community would also be very useful.' On working in court there was general consensus on the lack of proper time: 'We are under pressure to see people before ten and cannot always find the information we need in time.' 'The cut off at 3 p.m. is too abrupt – we lose some cases because of it.'

There were also constraints which meant that the systems followed were different from case to case: 'Occasionally the prosecutor is lobbied or negotiated with before court. Sometimes we speak to the defence. It would be more productive to hand the information to the court directly but this cannot always happen.'

For a system relying on the production of accurate information quickly it was not surprising to find that communication was an issue, as these comments testify: 'Police information is often lacking or incomplete.' 'There is a lack of feedback about second bail applications. There could be a better communication system between referrals.' 'Information on why bail is not given is not recorded.' 'There is no mechanism to forward information to the remand centres.' 'If the prison bail information officer has not seen a prisoner then there will be no information. This is a gap in the system. Computer records would be a good idea. We have no access to prison records from court.' 'There is rotten communication with the prison. A lot of information is not sent and we cannot send faxes because of security'.

Finally a few comments were made on improving the system. The police bail decisions, for example, were seen as inconsistent and yet were often binding because they were followed: 'Our job is more difficult because a lot of high-risk people are in court now that police bail is diverting low-risk people. There is no appeal against police bail.'

The role of the CPS was seen as too central: 'The CPS decides whether to use bail information or not. It would be better if it went directly to the court.' 'Sometimes the CPS uses bail information negatively.'

The major gap was seen as the lost opportunity between first remand in custody and second appearance in court, which was put down to poor communication systems and lack of commitment by prison staff: 'Very little is achieved by prison bail staff in a week.' 'There could be a better communication system between referrals. There is time there to set up a bail package that the court would support, but it is not used.' And again:

> There is no mechanism to forward information to the remand centres. It may go with the prisoner but not in every case. The prison bail information unit does not intervene in every case. Prisoners often decline to be interviewed, or so the form says, but this might be laziness on the part of the prison bail information officer.

Overall bail information officers valued their job despite the difficulties. Successes were described and overall positive comments made about the role: 'We are seen as objective and trusted. The system serves the hostel well. It is good for street drinkers. It is a link between the court and the resources in the community.'

The ACPOs' view

> Support for pre-trial and bail support.
> Operational decisions (in with court?).
> Partnership advantages and disadvantages.
> Research data needed.

The three ACPOs with line management responsibility for pre-trial services in their area had distinct philosophical stances on pre-trial work. One saw the advantage as being chiefly diversion from custody using 'positive bail information', and questioned the 'ethical correctness' of working intrusively with the unconvicted in bail support work. Another emphasized the separate importance of pre-trial work as a distinct and important part of the work of the probation service:

> We believe that bail work should be separate from court work, despite the thematic inspection recommendation that they should be combined. We think that if they are not separately constituted pre-trial work is likely to be lost because it is a low priority in a court team.

Three themes emerged from the interviews as being important in developing good pre-trial work: good feedback, good systems and good partnership. On feedback and evaluation there was consensus on its lack: 'We don't have clear research on bail information and what it means. It is hit and miss at the moment – officers make a judgement in good faith but more research is needed.' 'The main weakness is lack of research and lack of support from government. There is disproportionate imprisonment of black defendants, which we could use bail support to address. There is scope for more work there.'

Although one ACPO said optimistically that 'defining outcomes can be too restrictive; we have a partnership with shared aims and the outcome will follow', it was added that 'If the service has a weakness it is the lack of user feedback, a failure in evaluation on completion and a lack of rigour on breach.'

On systems a number of observations were made including the comment above that 'bail work should be separate from court work'. Communication was also questioned – 'whether information gets fed back to PSR authors' – and it was acknowledged that 'although there is a computerized record system not all records appear to be kept up to date'.

On value for money: 'We may make too many assumptions about the benign nature of our interventions and cut the service that we actually provide to individuals. The philosophy is about aggregated decisions but takes little account of actual cases.'

Finally, on partnership a number of views were expressed. There was some doubt: 'If I have a misgiving about partnership it would be that it might be losing us core work. Value for money asks us to identify and stick to our key tasks', but also more enthusiasm:

> We were providing through the partnership a number of aspects to a service that would not have been provided otherwise. In particular staff available twenty-four hours per day, familiar with the criminal justice system and able to use brief but critical interventions focused on young people.

Our partners were able to offer a service difficult for the statutory body to deliver. The partnership has been very good. With the 1986 funding we were able to provide a service that the Probation Service had difficulty in providing itself. They were more available and able to focus.

Bibliography

Ares, C. (1963). 'The Manhattan Bail Project', *New York University Law Review*, 67, 70–1.

Ashworth, A. (1992). *Sentencing in Criminal Justice*, London: Weidenfeld & Nicolson.

Ashworth, A. (1994). *The Criminal Process: An Evaluative Study*, Oxford: Oxford University Press.

Ashworth, A., Cavadino, P., Gibson, B., Harding, J., Rutherford, A., Seago, P. and Whyte, L. (1992). *The Youth Court*, Winchester: Waterside Press.

Audit Commission (1996). *Misspent Youth*, London: Audit Commission.

Baldwin, J. (1992). 'Preparing the record of taped interviews', *RCCJ Research Study No.2*, London: HMSO.

Beamer, S. (1991). 'The study of HMP Holloway Bail Unit – users' and staffs' perspectives', unpublished M.Sc. thesis, London (London School of Economics).

Bennetto, J. (1994). 'Defendants wait in prison for trial', *Independent*, 25 August 1994.

Blumental, S. and Wessley, S. (1992). 'National survey of current arrangements for diversion from custody in England and Wales', *British Medical Journal*, 305, 1322–5.

Brink, B. and Stone, C. (1988). 'Defendants who do not ask for bail', *Criminal Law Review*, 152–62.

Broderick, V. (1993). 'Pre-trial detention in the criminal justice process', *Federal Probation*, 57, No.1, 4–8.

Brown, D. (1998). *Offending on Bail and Police Use of Conditional Bail*, Home Office Research Directorate Paper 72, London: Home Office.

Buddress, L. (1997). 'Federal probation and pre-trial services – a cost-effective and successful community corrections system', *Federal Probation*, 61: 1, 5–12.

Burrows, J. (1993). 'Bail process: a composite narrative map', Bail Issues Steering Group.

Burrows, J., Henderson, P. and Morgan, P. (1994). *Improving Bail Decisions*, Home Office Research and Planning Unit Paper 90, London: Home Office.

Bynum, T. (1977). *An Empirical Exploration of the Factors Influencing Release on Recognisance*, Florida State University, School of Criminal Justice.

Cadigan, T. (1993). 'Technology and pre-trial services', *Federal Probation*, 57: 1, 48–53.

Carver, J. (1993). 'Using drug testing to reduce detention', *Federal Probation*, 57: 1, 42–6.

Cavadino, P. and Gibson, B. (1993). *Bail, the Law, Best Practice and the Debate*, Winchester: Waterside Press.

Clark, P. and Boyd, J. (1986). *Pre-trial Services in Michigan*, Michigan: Michigan Prison and Jail Overcrowding Project.

Collyer, A., Davies, G., Hensman, M. and Hutchins, J. (1993). *Approved Probation and Bail Hostels: A Report of a Thematic Inspection*, HM Inspectorate of Probation, London: Home Office.

Commission for Racial Equality (1990). *Bail Hostels and Racial Equality*, London: Commission for Racial Equality.

Devon Probation Service (1994). 'Bail support scheme proposal', internal document, Devon Probation Service in partnership with Ichthuse.

Doherty, M. J. and East, R. (1985). 'Bail decisions in magistrates' courts', *British Journal of Criminology*, 251–79.

Drakeford, M. (1999). *Privatisation and Social Policy*, London: Longman.

Fielding, N. and Fowles, T. (1990). 'Penal policy file No.37', *Howard Journal*, 29: 2, 130–42.

Flood-Page, C. and Mackie, A. (1998). *Sentencing Practice: An Examination of Decisions in Magistrates' Courts and the Crown Court in the Mid-1990s*, Home Office Research Study 180, London: Home Office.

Galvin, J. and Busher, W. (1977). *Instead of Jail*, vol.2: *Alternatives to Pretrial Detention*, Washington: National Institute of Law Enforcement and Criminal Justice.

Gibson, B. (1995). *Introduction to the Magistrates' Court*, Winchester: Waterside Press.

Godson, D. and Mitchell, C. (1991). *Bail Information Schemes in English Magistrates, Courts*, London: Inner London Probation Service.

Haines, K. and Drakeford, M. (1998). *Young People and Youth Justice*, Basingstoke: Macmillan.

Haines, K. and Octigan, M. (1999). *Reducing Remands in Custody: The Probation and Remand Services*, London: Association of Chief Officers of Probation.

Hardy, S. (1997). *A Study of Bail Hostels in the West Midlands 1993–96*, Birmingham: West Midlands Probation Service.

Harries, R. (1999). *The Cost of Criminal Justice*, London: Home Office Research Department.

Her Majesty's Inspectorate of Probation (1997a). *Probation and Partnership*, London: Home Office.

Her Majesty's Inspectorate of Probation (1997b). *Thematic Inspection of the Probation Service in the Crown and Magistrates' Court*, London: Home Office.

Her Majesty's Inspectorate of Probation (1998). *Delivering an Enhanced Level of Community Supervision: Report of a Thematic Inspection on the Work of Approved Probation and Bail Hostels*, London: Home Office.

Home Office (1991). 'Cash limits for probation services', Chief Probation Officers' Circular 23/91, London: Home Office.

Home Office (1992). *The Morgan Report*, London: Home Office.

Home Office (1999a). *National Bail Training Manual*, London: Home Office.

Home Office (1999b). *Action Plan for the Probation Service*, London: Home Office.

Home Office (2000a). Probation Circular 29/2000, London: Home Office.

Home Office (2000b). *Probation National Standards*, London: Home Office.

Home Office Draft Circular **/99. Bail Information Schemes.

186 BIBLIOGRAPHY

Home Office Research and Planning Unit (1988). *Bail and Probation Work: The ILPS Temporary Bail Action Project*, Paper 46, London: Home Office.

Home Office Research and Planning Unit (1990). *Bail and Probation Work II: The Use of London Probation Bail Hostels for Bailees*, Paper 50, London: Home Office.

Home Office Research and Statistics Directorate, *Research Findings No.72*, London: Home Office.

Hucklesby, A. (1997a). 'Remand decision-maker', *Criminal Law Reports*, 269–81.

Hucklesby, A. (1997b). 'Court culture: an explanation of variations in the use of bail by magistrates' courts', *The Howard Journal*, 36: 2, 129–45.

Hucklesby, A. and Marshall, E. (2000). 'Tackling offending on bail', *Howard Journal*, 39: 2, 150–70.

Hughes, J. and Henkel, K. (1997). 'The federal probation and pretrial services system since 1975: an era of growth and change', *Federal Probation*, 61: 1, 103–11.

Hughes, W. (1993). 'Foreword', *Federal Probation*, 57: 1.

Jarvis, G., Parker, H. and Sumner, M. (1987). 'An ambivalent service', *Probation Journal*, 34, 103–4.

Jefferson, T. and Walker, M. (1992). 'Ethnic minorities in the criminal justice system', *Criminal Law Reports*, 83.

Lewis, H. and Mair, G. (1988), *The Use of London Probation/Bail Hostels, Bail and Probation Work*, Home Office Research and Planning Unit, Paper 50, London: Home Office.

Lipsky, M. (1980). *Street-level Bureaucracy: Dilemmas of the Individual in Public Services*, New York: Russell Sage Foundation.

Lloyd, C. (1992). *Bail Information Schemes: Practices and Effect*, Home Office Research and Planning Unit Paper No. 69, London: Home Office.

Lord Chancellor's Department (LCD) (1999). 'Time intervals for criminal proceedings in magistrates' courts: October 1998', *Information Bulletin*, Issue 2/99.

McConville, M. and Hodgson, J. (1992). *Custodial Legal Advice and the Right to Silence*, RCCJ Research Study No.16, London: HMSO.

McConville, M., Hodgson, J., Bridges, L. and Pavlovic, A. (1994). *Standing Accused*, Oxford: Oxford University Press.

McConville, M., Sanders, A. and Leng, R. (1991). *The Case for the Prosecution*, London: Routledge.

McLean, I., Morrish, P. and Greenhill, J. (1995). *Magistrates' Court Index*, London: FT Law and Tax.

Matthews, W. (1998). 'Pretrial diversion: promises we can't keep', *Journal of Offender Counseling, Services and Rehabilitation*, 12: 2, 191–202.

Meyer, S. and Holloway, K. (1993). 'The Fastrack Program', *Federal Probation*, 57: 1, 36–41.

Morgan, P. and Henderson, P. (1998). *Remand Decisions and Offending on Bail: Evaluation of the Bail Process Project*, Home Office Research Study No.184, London: Home Office.

Murray, D. and Octigan, M. (1997). 'The effectiveness of bail information and bail support schemes', workshop paper given at the Howard League Conference, 'Positive Justice', New College, Oxford, 10 September 1997.

National Association for the Care and Resettlement of Offenders (NACRO) (1995). *Managing Remand*, London: NACRO.

NACRO (1993a). *Pre-trial Initiatives Paper 1*, London: NACRO.

NACRO (1993b). *Pre-trial Initiatives Paper 2: A Framework for Bail Support*, London: NACRO.

NACRO (1996). *The NACRO Bail Support Directory*, London: NACRO.

National Audit Office (1989). *Review of the Crown Prosecution Service*, London: HMSO.

Northamptonshire Probation Service (1996). 'Northampton Bail Support Programme Interim Statistics, April 1992–January 1993', unpublished internal report.

Nottingham, S. and Mitchell, C. (1994), *Bail Information Schemes in Prison, Review of Prison Service Agency Action Plan*, London: Home Office.

Payne G. (1989). 'Bail hostels: between bail and jail', *Probation Journal*, 36: 1, 37–40.

Penal Affairs Consortium (1995a). *Bail, the Law, Best Practice and the Debate*, London: Penal Affairs Consortium.

Penal Affairs Consortium (1995b). *Bail: Some Current Issues*, London: Penal Affairs Consortium.

Pratt, J. K. and Bray, K. (1985), 'Bail hostels: alternatives to custody?', *British Journal of Criminology*, 25: 2, 160–71.

Pritchard, C. and Cox, M. (1996). *A Two Year Evaluation of Bail Support Schemes Contributing to the Reduction of Crime and Enhancement of the Community*, Dorchester: Dorset Probation Service.

Pryor, D. and Smith, W. (1982). *Pretrial Issues: Significant Research Findings Concerning Pretrial Release*, Washington, DC: Pretrial Resource Center.

Raine, J. and Willson, M. (1995). *Conditional Bail or Bail with Conditions?*, Inlogov, University of Birmingham.

Raine, J. and Willson, M. (1996). 'The imposition of conditions in bail decisions: from summary punishment to better behaviour on remand', *Howard Journal*, 35: 3, 256–70.

Raynor, P., Smith, D. and Vanstone, M. (1994). *Effective Probation Practice*, London: Macmillan.

Renzema, M. and Skelton, D. (1991). 'The scope of electronic monitoring today', *Journal of Offender Monitoring*, 4: 4, 6–11.

Saunders, A. (1994). 'From suspect to trial', in M. Maguire, R. Morgan, and R. Reiner, *The Oxford Handbook of Criminology*, Oxford: Clarendon Press, 773–818.

Shaw, R. and Haines, K. (1989). *The Criminal Justice Systems: A Central Role for the Probation Service*, Cambridge Institute of Criminology.

Simon, F. and Wilson, S. (1975). *Fielding Bail Hostel: The First Nine Months*, Home Office Research Study No.30, London: Home Office.

Smartt, U. (1997). 'John Howard or Woolf: who was better for remands?', Paper presented at the Fifteenth Annual Conference of the Howard League for Penal Reform, 9–10 September 1997, New College, Oxford.

Smith, G. (1994). Speech to Pre-trial Services Conference, Lincoln.

Stone C. (1988), *Bail Information for the Crown Prosecution Service*, vol. 1 of the Final Report on the Probation Initiative, London: Vera Institute of Justice.

Stone, C. (1989). *Public Interest and Case Assessment*, vol. 2 of the Final Report on the Probation Initiative, 'Diversion from Custody and Prosecution', London: Vera Institute of Justice.

Thomas, W. (1976). *Bail Reform in America*, Berkeley: University of California Press.

Tjoflat, G. (1983). Prepared statement to the hearing before the Subcommittee on Crime of the Committee on the Judiciary House of Representatives, Serial No. 60.

Toboloswky, P. and Quinn, J. (1993). 'Pretrial release in the 1990s: Texas takes another look at nonfinancial release conditions', *New England Journal on Criminal and Civil Confinement*, 19: 2, 267–327.

Toborg, M. (1982). *Pretrial Release: A National Evaluation of Practices and Outcomes*, Washington, DC: National Institute of Justice.

US Congress (1983). Hearing before the Subcommittee on Crime of the Committee on the Judiciary House of Representatives, Serial No.60.

Vanstone, M. (1988). 'Values, leadership and the future of the Probation Service', *Probation Journal*, 35: 4, 131–4.

Visher, C. (1992). 'Pretrial drug testing', *National Institute of Justice Research in Brief*, September 1992.

Warner, S. and McIvor, G. (1994). *Pre-trial Services in Scotland: An Evaluation of Two Experimental Bail Information and Accommodation Schemes*, Edinburgh: Scottish Office Central Research Unit.

West Midlands Probation Service (WMPS) (1997a). *Bail Support Annual Report*, Birmingham: West Midlands Probation Service.

West Midlands Probation Service (1997b). *Pre-trial Service Department Statistics*, Birmingham: West Midlands Probation Service.

West Midlands Probation Service (1999a). *Annual Report on Bail Support*, Birmingham, West Midlands Probation Service.

West Midlands Probation Service (1999b). *Audit of Offender Accommodation*, Birmingham: West Midlands Probation Service.

White, K. and Brody, S. (1980). 'The use of bail hostels', *Criminal Law Review*, 420–5.

White, P. (1999). 'The prison population in 1998: a statistical review', *Home Office Research, Development and Statistics Directorate Research Findings,* No.94, London: Home Office.

White, P. and Woodbridge, J. (1998). 'The prison population in 1997', *Home Office Statistical Bulletin*, Issue 5/98, London: Home Office.

Wice, P. (1972). *Bail and its Reform: A National Survey*, Chicago: University of Illinois.

Williams, B. (1992). *Bail Information: An Evaluation of the Scheme at HMP Moorland*, Bradford: Haughton Publishing Ltd.

Wilson, D. and Ashton, J. (1998), *What Everyone in Britain should Know about Crime and Punishment*, London: Blackstone Press Ltd.

Zander, M. (1971). 'The study of bail and custody decisions in London magistrates' courts', *Criminal Law Review*, 197–211.

Index